WINTER NATURE NOTES
FOR
NOVA SCOTIANS

WINTER NATURE NOTES
FOR
NOVA SCOTIANS

by

Merritt A. Gibson

Illustration by

Twila L. Robar

LANCELOT PRESS

Hantsport, Nova Scotia

ACKNOWLEDGMENT

This book has been published with the assistance of the Nova Scotia Department of Culture, Recreation and Fitness.

ISBN 0-88999-122-7

Published 1980

LANCELOT PRESS LIMITED, Hantsport, N.S.
Office and plant situated on Highway No. 1,½ mile east of Hantsport

CONTENTS

INTRODUCTION

Nature Notes has been compiled for the many Nova Scotians who enjoy the outdoors in winter. If you are a cross-country skier or a snowshoer, a winter camper, or simply someone who likes to wander along the winter roads and woodlands trails, you have a wonderful opportunity to observe nature. As you travel quietly through the woods, across farmlands, along streams and over marshlands, you can unobtrusively watch the birds and mammals, learn to identify the trees and larger shrubs, be introduced to a variety of habitats, and gain some appreciation for their characteristics and values. Indeed, as your interest in nature develops, you may plan trips to areas of special interest: over farmlands to count pheasants and partridges, along a rapidly flowing river to search for mergansers and goldeneye ducks, or through the woods to an "eagle-tree" overlooking an escarpment. Undertaking trips with such aims in mind will add a new dimension to your enjoyment of the outdoors in wintertime.

Winter is a good time to start nature watching. There are fewer species of birds than in the summer but the number is sufficient to present a challenge for the beginner and the confusing immature and fall plumages seen in the summer and autumn woods are absent. Many trees and shrubs have lost their leaves but characteristics of the bark and buds may be used to identify them. Winter is one of the best times to hunt for mammals. Mammals are common in the Nova Scotian woods, but many are shy and difficult for the beginner to find at any time of the year. In winter, however, tracks provide a record of the animals which live in the woods and fields. It takes patience and practice to learn to identify tracks and to determine what the animal was doing and where it lives.

Nature Notes is intended to help you identify the common birds, trees and shrubs, and mammals that are present in Nova Scotia during the winter. If you begin watching nature in winter you will develop a good background to which you may add as you travel along the hiking trails and beaches in summer. You will begin a fascinating hobby that will give you many hours of enjoyment for as many years as you wish to pursue it.

BIRDS

Many people have taken up bird watching as a hobby. Nova Scotia has a large variety of birds and you will enjoy learning to recognize the more common species and learning something about their habits. Bird watching takes you outdoors, to many habitats in search of different kinds of birds. There is a challenge and satisfaction in finding a species for the first time, in indentifying a bird you have never seen before, and in adding it to your "life list". With a knowledge of birds you will anticipate the changing seasons and look forward to the arrival of new species. Bird watching is a pleasant and enjoyable hobby. It makes you aware of the outdoors and of the many beauties of nature.

All that is needed to find birds is curiosity and patience. A pair of binoculars will help you see birds at a distance or in the tree tops and a "Field Guide" will help you name them. You can find birds everywhere, but larger numbers and greater varieties occur in certain habitats. More variety can be found along the borders of woods and in open woods of young growth than in the deeper, mature woods. Thickets around swamps and open water are among the best bird areas. Hedgerows and weedy areas around fields and along fences provide berries and seeds for many kinds of birds, and the coast and saltwater marshlands have species that are different from those found in the fields and woodlands.

About 400 species of birds have been seen in Nova Scotia. Some of these are strays perhaps blown in during storms, others are not common but occur regularly, and most are present only during the summer or seen during the spring and fall migrations. About 100 species have been reported during the winter months, and about 50 are described in *Nature Notes*. These birds were selected because they are common and will likely be seen, or although they are less common their colours and habits are such that the occasional sighting is an exciting one, or because the interested observer may wish to search for a particular species and with patience and time can find the ones included.

This section includes a "Quick Guide" that groups the birds on the basis of size and overall colour. It is intended to help the beginner by limiting his search through the book to several possible species. The identification can then be made with the help of the illustrations.

8

As you become familiar with the major bird groups you will soon be able to turn directly to the appropriate section of the book without using the "Quick Guide". Always read the descriptions and remember that there are many species of birds in Nova Scotia which are not included in *Nature Notes*. As you pursue bird watching you will certainly find these less common birds and you will then need a more complete "Field Guide".

QUICK GUIDE TO THE BIRDS

This "Quick Guide" divides birds on the basis of size and colour and refers you to a section of *Nature Notes* where by searching only a few plates you will find the bird in question. Three size groups are used: Sparrow size (15 to 17 cm), Robin size (25 to 26 cm), and Crow size (46 to 48 cm)

A. Larger than a crow	Bird or Group	Page
Mostly Black	Black Duck	12
	White-winged Scoter	15
	Raven	36
Mostly Black and White	Common Goldeneye	13
	Common Eider	14
	Common Merganser	16
	Bald Eagle	20
	Great Black-backed Gull	24
Mostly White	Herring Gull	25
	Snowy Owl	31
Mostly Brown	Common Eider	14
	White-winged Scoter	15
	Hawks	17
	Immature Bald Eagle	20
	Common Pheasant	22
	Immature Gulls	24
	Owls	29

B. Crow size or slightly smaller		
Mostly Black	Crow	36
Mostly Brown	Sharp-shinned Hawk	17
	Ruffed Grouse	21
	Grey Partridge	23
Mostly Grey (and various colours)	Pigeon	27
Mostly Steel Blue	Sharp-shinned Hawk	17
Mostly White	Black Guillemot	26

11

DUCKS

About 30 species of ducks have been sighted in the waters of Nova Scotia. Many of these are summer or only occasional visitors. Five species are included in *Nature Notes,* ones that might be encountered during the winter in marine bays or open fresh-water habitats.

BLACK DUCK
(Anas rubripes)

Description
- large, 50 to 60 cm
- dark brown or dusky black, head and underneath lighter, purple wing patch
- undersurfaces of wings show white during flight

Habitat
- coastal waters and marshes, rivers and lakes with open water, flooded farmlands

Notes
- The Black Duck is our most common duck. It swims on the surface and feeds by "tipping" to reach submerged plants, roots and shellfish. The Black Duck seldom dives and does not usually swim underwater. It springs into flight directly from the water, and does not run along the surface as do many ducks. Its voice is a loud, repeated "quacking".

12

COMMON GOLDENEYE
(Bucephala clangula)

Description
- large, 40 to 60 cm
- male: dark green head, black back, white underparts, circular white patch between eye and bill, black wings with conspicuous white areas in flight
- female: brown head, back and wings grey, white underparts

Habitat
- coastal waters, estuaries, open rivers and lakes, especially those with rapids or fast moving water

Notes
- The Common Goldeneye is so-named because of the deep yellow colour of its eye. It is a diving duck and feeds on fish, shellfish and plants. It may remain submerged for up to 30 seconds and may dive to a depth of 3 metres, although longer and deeper dives have been reported. On the bottom it may overturn stones with its beak in search for insect larvae and other aquatic animals. It usually runs along the water for a short distance before taking flight. In flight it shows a compact body, a short neck and a large head. This contrasts with the elongate form and long neck shown by many ducks. Its rapid wing beats produce a whistling sound, hence the nickname "Whistler".

13

COMMON EIDER
(Somateria mollissima)

Description
- large, heavy duck; about 50 to 60 cm
- males: back and breast white; head white with black crown and green patch on nape; sides, belly and tail black
- females and immatures: brown barred with black

Habitat
- along coast, especially around rocky islands

Notes
- The Common Eider is frequently seen in small flocks. Occasionally the flocks combine to form huge rafts. It is a diving duck and usually dives to a depth of 2 m and may remain submerged for up to 30 seconds. However, much deeper dives and dives lasting almost 2 minutes have been reported. The Eider feeds on whole molluscs and crustaceans, grinding the shells with powerful gizzards. Eiders usually fly in a line or semi-circle low over the water. Its wing beat is slow and it often shows a flight pattern of alternating wing beats and glides. The down of Eider nests, which is formed of the plucked inner feathers of the breast, is noted for its softness and is of commercial value for insulation, filling pillows, etc. The King Eider is also found along the Nova Scotian coast but usually stays offshore during winter and seldom will be seen. The male may be distinguished from the Common Eider by its white crown and by its beak which extends up over the forehead as a large, orange shield (comb duck).

WHITE-WINGED SCOTER
(Melanitta deglandi)

Description
- large, slender duck; about 50 cm
- male; mostly black, white crescent under eye, white wing patch which is most evident during flight
- female and immature: greyish-brown, lighter below and behind eye, white wing patch

Habitat
- common along coast, especially in leeward shoals around rocky islands

Notes
- The White-winged Scoter winters along the Atlantic coast, arriving during the early autumn and leaving in March and April for its breeding grounds in the Northwest Territories. A few remain in Nova Scotian waters during the summer. It is a diving duck, diving to considerable depths and using its legs and wings to swim under water. It also makes repeated shallow dives. The Scoter feeds on molluscs and crustaceans which it swallows whole. It grinds their shells within its muscular gizzard and swallows small stones to assist in this grinding. Scoters fly in a long line, low over the water. The black scoter and the surf scoter are also present along the Nova Scotian coast, the former being most numerous during the spring and fall migrations. Neither one is commonly seen in the winter.

15

COMMON MERGANSER
(Mergus merganser)

Description
- large, 50 to 70 cm
- male: dark green head, black back and wings, greyish rump and tail, white underparts, white patches on wings close to body and most conspicuous during flight
- female: brown head with crest; grey back, wings and tail; white underparts
- bill long with sawtoothed edge and hooked tip

Habitat
- coastal waters, open lakes and rivers, especially those with fast moving water

Notes
- The Common Merganser is also called the Shelldrake or Sawbill. It is often found with Goldeneyes. The Merganser is a diving duck and can swim underwater in pursuit of prey. In small flocks they will often dive in sequence, one following the other. It feeds on fish such as eels, and the sawtoothed and hooked bill is adapted for catching and holding prey. Mergansers run along the water with head and neck out-stretched when taking flight. In flight they are long, slender, black and white ducks that fly in a line low above the water. The Red-breasted Merganser is also present in Nova Scotia during the winter. The male may be distinguished from the Common Merganser by its crested head and a broad reddish-brown band across the breast. Both species are present in fresh water and marine habitats. However, the Common Merganser will be seen more frequently on fresh water and the Red-breasted Merganser is found more commonly along the coast.

HAWKS and EAGLES

About 14 species of hawks have been observed in Nova Scotia. Three of these are frequently seen during winter and these together with the Bald Eagle are included in *Nature Notes*.

SHARP-SHINNED HAWK
(Accipiter striatus)

Description
- small hawk, male up to 30 cm, female up to 35 cm
- upperparts steel-blue, underparts white barred with reddish-brown, tail long and barred
- immatures and females more brownish

Habitat
- open woods, bush land, around villages and towns

Notes
- The Sharp-shinned Hawk is the most common hawk in Nova Scotia during winter. It frequents the shrubbery about gardens and bird feeders from which it darts to catch small birds. It flies with a series of quick wing strokes and short glides. It seldom soars. In flight its wings are short and rounded and its tail is long and narrow. The Sharp-shinned Hawk eats fresh meat only, never carrion.

17

RED-TAILED HAWK
(Buteo jamaicensis)

Description
- large, male 50 to 55 cm, female 50 to 60 cm
- upperparts brown, throat and breast white, abdomen white streaked with brown, upper surface of tail is red in adult birds and barred in immature birds (tail becomes red in second year)

Habitat
- heavily wooded areas, dykelands, farmlands

Notes
- The Red-tailed Hawk is usually seen soaring in wide circles. In flight, it has broad rounded wings and a short fanned tail. Although the red is on the upper surface of the tail, it may shine through and be identified from below or the red may be seen when the tail is tilted to change directions. The Red-tailed Hawk feeds on mice and other small mammals which it finds in meadows, farmlands and around waste disposal areas. Most of its hunting is done from an elevated perch at the forest edge.

Dark Phase

Light Phase

ROUGH-LEGGED HAWK
(Buteo lagopus)

Description
- large, up to 60 cm, wing span over 120 cm
- shows light and dark phases
- light phase: brown above, breast cream coloured streaked with brown, complete dark brown band across abdomen, tail white with dark terminal band, undersurface of wing light with wrist and posterior border dark
- dark phase: dark brown, white showing at base of tail, undersurface of wing dark anteriorly and light with a dark border posteriorly

Habitat
- soaring or hovering over meadowlands and open or bush country

Notes
- The Rough-legged Hawk is most often seen in flight. In flight, it has broad rounded wings and a fanned tail. It is the only large winter hawk that hovers. In the light phase, it shows light and dark areas and a characteristic broad dark band across the abdomen. In the dark phase, it appears all dark with white at the base of its tail and along the posterior wing surface. The Rough-legged Hawk is one of our most beneficial hawks, feeding largely on mice, which it captures in their runways through the snow.

19

Immature

BALD EAGLE
(Haliaestus leucocephalus)

Description
- our largest bird, up to 110 cm, wing span up to 2.5 m
- adults nearly black, white head and tail
- juveniles, during first 3 years, dark brown, with scattered white-streaking
- first-year young appear larger than adults

Habitat
- along coast, open lakes, and river valleys

Notes
- The Bald Eagle feeds primarily on carrion and fish and is frequently seen patrolling a river or soaring near open water or waste disposal areas. Often it perches majestically in a tree overlooking a river valley or on a mountainside. Such "eagle trees" are known where eagles have been found for more than 20 years. The Eagle was once more numerous and more widely distributed in North America than it is at present. Its numbers have been reduced primarily by the spread of civilization and the widespread use of pesticides. Nova Scotia now has one of the largest populations of eagles in eastern North America and these magnificent birds must be protected.

20

GROUSE, PHEASANTS and PARTRIDGES

The Spruce Grouse and the Ruffed Grouse are native to Nova Scotia. The Ring-necked Pheasant and the Grey Partridge have been successfully introduced and several attempts have been made to introduce Ptarmigan. The following three species are the ones most frequently observed.

RUFFED GROUSE
(Bonasa umbellus)

Description
- about the size of a crow
- upperparts brown and grey mottled with black and white
- underparts lighter and barred with brown; tail reddish-brown,
- barred black ruff on sides of neck

Habitat
- wooded areas, particularly young growth woodlands

Notes
- The Ruffed Grouse or "Partridge" is usually found in deep thickets and sheltered swamps, especially where birch, poplar and hemlock are common. It feeds on the buds and twigs of trees and on berries and other small fruit. When flushed, the Ruffed Grouse springs into the air with a roar of wings, that startles the observer. By rapidly beating its wings against the air the Ruffed Grouse produces the "drumming" sound heard throughout the woodlands in the spring and fall. The spruce grouse is also resident in Nova Scotia. The male can be distinguished from the Ruffed Grouse by its black chin, throat and breast. The female is brown barred with greys and black. It lives in deep coniferous forests where it feeds on the buds and young growth of spruce and firs.

21

RING-NECKED PHEASANT
(Phasianus colchicus)

Description
- about twice as long as a crow
- male: copper coloured with patterns of red, green, black and white-tipped feathers; crown green with black ear tufts; neck with white collar; pointed tail up to 50 cm long
- female: smaller, more greyish brown, long tail

Habitat
- bushes and thickets surrounding farm fields and orchards

Notes
- The Ring-necked Pheasant, native to China, was successfully introduced in Nova Scotia in 1935. It is now established but domestically raised birds are released each year to help maintain its numbers. Pheasants feed on grain, weed seeds, berries and other small fruit. In rural areas it is a frequent visitor to bird feeders that provide chicken "scratch".

GREY PARTRIDGE
(Perdix perdix)

Description
- smaller than a crow
- greyish-brown speckled with black; sides, lower back, and tail reddish, the latter best seen in flight
- underparts grey speckled with black, red-brown on belly

Habitat
- open fields, dykeland

Notes
- Grey or Hungarian Partridges, or "Huns", were successfully introduced in Nova Scotia from Europe on several occasions between 1926 and 1934. They are now well established but domestically raised birds are released periodically to help maintain their numbers. Huns are found on the ground, not perched in bushes or trees, usually where the wind has swept the snow clear or where tufts of grass protrude through the snow. They tunnel into the snow for protection against winter storms and to seek food. They feed on grain and green grass. They are often seen in small coveys of 4 to 12 birds. These coveys are usually family groups that remain together during the winter period.

GULLS

Seven species of gulls are found regularly in Nova Scotia during the winter months. The two types described below are among our most common birds.

immature

GREAT BLACK-BACKED GULL
(Larus marinus)

Description
- much larger than a crow
- white, black back and upper wings
- juveniles, first 3 years, grey mottled with brown; can be distinguished from other juvenile gulls by larger size

Habitat
- coastal and ranging inland over farm fields and open bodies of water

Notes
- The Great Black-backed Gull is the largest common gull in Nova Scotia and the only one with a black back. It scavenges along the beaches and rivers and, especially during winter, frequents waste disposal areas. Between feedings, they may roost in open fields in flocks of several hundred birds.

24

immature

HERRING GULL
(Larus argentatus)

Description
- larger than a crow
- white, bluish-grey back and wings, black wing tips with white spots
- juveniles, first 3 years, grey mottled with brown

Habitat
- coastal and ranging inland over farm fields and open bodies of water

Notes
- The Herring Gull is the most common gull in Nova Scotia. It is a scavenger along beaches and rivers, and about waste disposal areas. In summer it follows the farmer's tractor when plowing or mowing and feeds on the grubs, insects and mice. It is the Herring Gull that follows ships and fishing vessels out to sea, and scavenges the refuse thrown overboard. In winter they may form large roosting colonies of several hundred birds and often roost with the Great Black-backed Gulls.

GUILLEMOT

Guillemots, Auks, Puffins, Murres and Dovekies make up a group of birds called the Auks. Six species are found along the coast of Nova Scotia but they usually remain far out to sea during the winter. The Black Guillemot, however, is regularly seen and is included in *Nature Notes*. Murres and Dovekies are also occasionally present inshore, especially following a storm. They are described later in the section entitled "Other Birds to Look For".

BLACK GUILLEMOT
(Cepphus grylle)

Description
- small bird, about pigeon size
- underparts white, back dark and mottled with white and brown, white wing patch, wing tips black, legs and feet red

Habitat
- inshore and rocky coastal waters, primarily along Atlantic and lower Bay of Fundy coasts

Notes
- The Black Guillemot in summer plumage is all black with a large, white wing patch, thus its name. The Black Guillemot breeds in Nova Scotia, laying its eggs in crevices and hollows in rocky cliffs. It is a diving bird, swims rapidly, and is able to travel considerable distances underwater using both its feet and wings. Guillemots feed on crustaceans and small fish including eels.

26

PIGEONS AND DOVES

Two species of pigeons and doves are present in Nova Scotia, the common Pigeon or Rock Dove and the Mourning Dove. Both species are frequently seen during the winter.

PIGEON
(Columba livia)

Description
- smaller than a crow
- various colours, white rump, most show bluish-grey with purplish or iridescent tinge along back and shoulders; flocks often include birds which are predominantly white or brown

Habitat
- near civilization, cultivated fields near homes, city buildings
- rarely in remote areas or deep woodlands

Notes
- The Pigeon, or Rock Dove, was introduced from Europe. It occurs in flocks near civilization and feeds on seeds and waste. The variety of colours recalls the domestic period of its history when colour hybrids were selected and bred. All colours are descendant from the European Rock Dove. The wing beats are rapid and may produce a whistling sound. Often, the wings slap together when the birds are taking flight. In flight Pigeons glide with wings held high in a "V" shape.

27

MOURNING DOVE
(Zenaidura macroura)

Description
- larger than a robin
- upperparts greyish or light brown, neck with purplish tinge
- underparts buff coloured with reddish tinge
- tail long, tapered and pointed, slate-grey with white sides

Habitat
- feeding primarily in cultivated fields, resting in trees or on power lines

Notes
- The Mourning Dove occurs more frequently in some winters that in others. It is usually found in flocks ranging in size from 3 or 4 birds to more than 50. It feeds on weed seeds, berries or nuts and often visits bird feeders. Their name is derived from the soft, plaintive call which is more frequently heard in the spring and summer than in the winter. In flight, the wing beats are rapid and produce a whistling sound which, along with the white outer tail feathers, provides a means of identifying it.

28

OWLS

Six species of Owls occur regularly in Nova Scotia during the winter period. Three of these are sufficiently common that the careful observer might see or hear them and are included in *Nature Notes*.

GREAT HORNED OWL
(Bubo virginianus)

Description
- a large owl, 55 to 60 cm; wing span about 1.5 m
- upperparts brown mottled with greys and black, conspicuous "ear" tufts or horns
- underparts paler, frequently rufous, and barred with greys and black, white throat patch which is more conspicuous in some individuals than in others

Habitat
- heavy timber, hunting into surrounding area at night

Notes
- The Great Horned Owl is a common owl in the Nova Scotia forest. It hunts primarily at night, feeding on mice and other small mammals and birds. It is generally inactive during the daytime. The Great Horned Owl is also called the Big Hoot Owl and its hoots are heard during the evening before midnight. While it may give from 3 to 6 low pitched "whoo's", it frequently gives 2 long followed by 2 short "whoo's".

29

BARRED OWL
(Strix varia)

Description
- a large owl, about 45 cm; wing span about 1 m
- upperparts brown mottled with greys and white, no ear tufts
- underparts white broadly barred with dark brown on upper breast
- eyes dark

Habitat
- deep woods, especially around lakes and swamps

Notes
- The Barred Owl is the most common owl in Nova Scotia. It is a nocturnal hunter, feeding primarily on mice and other small mammals. It is also known as the Hoot Owl. Its call is more accented than that of the Great Horned Owl and frequently consists of 8 "whoo's" with the last syllable dropping whoo — whoo — who — whoo — whoo — whoo — who — whooaaah —

30

SNOWY OWL
(Nyctea scandiaca)

Description
- a large owl, 60 cm; wing span about 1.5 m
- white, barred with black, no ear tufts

Habitat
- meadowlands, especially dykelands around the Minas Basin and upper Bay of Fundy

Notes
- The Snowy Owl is a winter visitor from the Arctic, and is fairly common in some winters and absent in others. Its visits peak in cycles of about 4 years and appear to be caused by periodic food shortages in the Arctic. Unlike most Nova Scotian owls, it hunts in the daytime. It feeds on small mammals and birds. The more heavily barred birds are the female and younger ones, the older males are mostly white.

31

WOODPECKERS

Only 2 species of woodpeckers, the Hairy Woodpecker and the Downy Woodpecker, are common in Nova Scotia during the winter. They are similar in plumage and habits and are considered together.

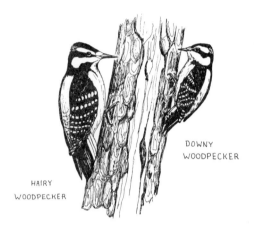

HAIRY WOODPECKER

DOWNY WOODPECKER

HAIRY WOODPECKER DOWNY WOODPECKER
(Dendrocopos villosus)   *(Dendrocopos pubescens)*

Description
- Downy Woodpecker is the smaller, about the size of a large sparrow; Hairy Woodpecker is larger, about the size of a robin
- both have a black back with a broad white centre stripe; wings black with white spots, tail black with white border, white breast
- bill of Hairy Woodpecker is proportionally longer and thicker than that of Downy Woodpecker; outer tail feathers all white in Hairy Woodpecker and white with black bars in Downy Woodpecker
- males have red spot on back of head

Habitat
- both species in open deciduous woods, shrubs, and especially alder thickets
- in winter, both frequent gardens and winter feeders for suet

Notes
- Both Downy and Hairy Woodpeckers are invaluable to the gardener, farmer, and forester. They work over trees and probe beneath the bark for hibernating insects, insect eggs and pupae, or they chisel with their sharp beaks into the tree for wood-boring larvae. Downy Woodpeckers are one of the natural controls of the corn borer and will often be seen, usually in pairs, working along the rows of corn stubble in winter fields.

LARKS

The Horned Lark is the only member of the lark family present in Nova Scotia.

HORNED LARK
(Eremophila alpestris)

Description
- size of large sparrow
- upperparts reddish-brown with black streaks, tail black bordered with white
- underparts whitish, throat and line above eye yellow, black line from bill to eye, black necklace, small black tufts back of eye

Habitat
- on ground in open fields, frequently near coast; especially common on dykelands around Minas Basin and upper Bay of Fundy

Notes
- The Horned Lark is so-called because the black tufts appear like horns. They walk or run along the ground, they do not hop as do many other ground birds, and they seldom perch in bushes or trees. They are frequently seen in small flocks, often mingled with snow buntings, feeding on weed seeds. They often congregate along highways in agricultural districts where they feed on waste grain blown from agricultural vehicles and pick up particles of gravel to assist grinding the seeds for digestion.

JAYS, CROWS and RAVENS

The jay and crow family is represented in Nova Scotia by the Blue Jay, Grey Jay, Crow, and Raven. All four are present during the winter

BLUE JAY
(Cyanocitta cristata)

Description
- slightly larger than a Robin
- head crest and back violet-blue, tail and wings blue with black and white bars
- underparts white with a black necklace

Habitat
- common, open woods, orchards, gardens

Notes
- The Blue Jay is one of our most familiar and colourful winter birds. Its "jay-jay-jay" throughout the woodlands and gardens is a well-known winter call. The Blue Jay feeds mainly on seeds, fruit and nuts. It is a common visitor to bird feeders offering sunflower seeds and suet. In summer Blue Jays usually withdraw into the deeper woods where nesting takes place, although a few may remain about homes and nest in garden conifers and shrubbery.

34

GREY JAY
(Perisorsus canadensis)

Description
- larger than a robin
- back and tail grey, face and throat white, dark cap on back of head, undersides ash grey

Habitat
- remote coniferous woods

Notes
- The Grey Jay is also called Canada Jay, Whiskey Jack, and Camp Robber. It is most common in deep woods in the interior of the province, and less common along the coastal regions, open farming areas, or near civilization. It is a frequent and popular visitor to campsites, flitting quietly into camp as soon as the fire and cooking have started. It is friendly and will readily accept handouts of food, or steal the food when the camper is not on guard.

CROW

RAVEN

CROW
(Corvus brachyrhynchos)

RAVEN
(Corvus corax)

Description
- large birds, Crow about 45 cm, Raven about 65 cm
- both birds entirely black
- Raven distinguished from Crow by its much larger size, by its hoarse "croak" in comparison with the "caw" of the Crow, and by its tail which in flight is wedge-shaped while that of the Crow is rounded

Habitat
- common throughout, showing a preference for farming and coastal regions

Notes
- Crows and Ravens are omnivores, feeding on seeds and fruits, waste from farms, sea life washed up along the shore, and on animals killed along the highways. In winter Crows often roost in rookeries and thousands may be seen flying from all directions into the rookery at dusk. When feeding in fields, a single Crow will give an alarm as someone approaches, alerting all of them into flight. A group of crows will often harass a hawk or dive into a tree where an owl is perched. Watch the Raven in the air, especially when there are two or more. They play games and are capable of performing many acrobatic manoeuvers, including aerial rolls and somersaults.

CHICKADEES, NUTHATCHES and CREEPERS

Five species of these three families are present in Nova Scotia. All five are frequently observed during the winter.

BLACK-CAPPED CHICKADEE
(Parus atricapillus)

BOREAL CHICKADEE
(Parus hudsonicus)

Description
- smaller than a sparrow
- upperparts greyish, underparts white, sides brownish, throat black
- Black-capped Chickadee: black cap
- Boreal Chickadee: brown cap

Habitat
- Black-capped Chickadee: everywhere, more common in open woods and gardens, and at winter feeders offering suet and sunflower seeds
- Boreal Chickadee: coniferous woods

Notes
- The Black-capped Chickadee is one of our best known winter birds. Its "chick-a-dee-dee" is clearly heard throughout the winter woods and gardens. Its summer song of 2 clear notes, the first high and the second low, described as "fee-bee" or "spring's here", may be heard after mid-February. The "chick-a-dee-dee" of the Boreal Chickadee is harsher and more nasal. Watch the antics of the Chickadees as they work their way around branches searching for hibernating insects and eggs. The "tsee-tsee" call is a "contact signal", helping to keep the flock together. A flock of Chickadees has several feeding sites that it visits each day and, consequently, Chickadees are often seen in the same places. The Boreal Chickadee is chiefly found in conifers, often in company with kinglets.

WHITE-BREASTED
NUTHATCH

RED-BREASTED
NUTHATCH

WHITE-BREASTED NUTHATCH
(Sitta carolinensis)
RED-BREASTED NUTHATCH
(Sitta canadensis)

Description
- about sparrow size
- upperparts bluish-grey, black cap
- White-breasted Nuthatch: underparts and cheeks white,
- reddish-brown under tail; outer tail and wing feathers black bordered with white
- Red-breasted Nuthatch: underparts reddish-brown, black line through eye

Habitat
- woodlands, orchards, gardens
- White-breasted Nuthatch: primarily in deciduous trees
- Red-breasted Nuthatch: primarily in conifers

Notes
- Nuthatches scamper over the tree "right-side-up and upside-down" looking for spiders, hibernating insects, eggs and larvae. They are the only birds that climb down a tree "head-first". The Red-breasted Nuthatch also feeds on the seeds of coniferous cones, and the White-breasted Nuthatch is a visitor to winter feeders offering suet and sunflower seeds. The call of both species is a nasal "ank-ank-ank" and is frequently heard throughout the woodlands. The voice of the Red-breasted Nuthatch is more highly pitched than that of the White-breasted Nuthatch.

38

BROWN CREEPER
(Certhia familiaris)

Description
  - smaller than a sparrow
  - upperparts brown and streaked, breast white, bill long and curved downward

Habitat
  - woodlands, occasionally garden trees and orchards

Notes
  - The Brown Creeper is the only small brown bird in Nova Scotia that climbs around the trunks of trees. Often it starts at the foot of the trunk and creeps upward in a spiral pattern and then darts to the foot of an adjacent tree. It searches under the bark with its curved beak for hibernating insects, spiders, and eggs. When danger approaches, it presses tightly against the tree and its brown and white colouration provides a good camouflage against the trunk.

THRUSHES

Of the six species of thrushes which occur regularly in Nova Scotia during the summer months, only the Robin is present during the winter.

winter

ROBIN
(Turdus migratorius)

Description
- about 25 cm
- upperparts black and greyish-black
- underparts brick red, throat white and black striped

Habitat
- in winter, sheltered areas, often bushes near swamps or along streams, orchards

Notes
- The Robin is perhaps our best known summer bird. It is less common in winter but may be found either singly or in small flocks of 4 to more than 20 birds. It feeds on berries and frozen fruit. Most of the Robins that nest here in summer migrate to the southern United States for winter and the winter Robins are usually those that nested in more northern latitudes.

40

KINGLETS

Two species of kinglets are present in Nova Scotia. The Ruby-crowned Kinglet is present only during the summer. The Golden-crowned Kinglet is resident throughout the year and is frequently seen in the winter woods.

GOLDEN-CROWNED KINGLET
(Regulus satrapa)

Description
- much smaller than a sparrow
- upperparts dark olive-grey; crown orange in male, yellow in female, bordered in both with a black stripe; white wing bar
- underparts olive-grey

Habitat
- chiefly coniferous woods

Notes
- The Golden-crowned Kinglet is our smallest winter bird. It is usually found in small flocks flitting, "chickadee-style", over the ends of conifer boughs searching for insects. It is often accompanied by chickadees. Its call, "Tsee-Tsee-Tsee", is a signal by which the members of the flock maintain contact with one another. It may be easily imitated by whistling through the teeth and the birds can be "lured" to the lower branches for easier observation.

STARLINGS and BLACKBIRDS

Seven species of starlings, blackbirds and orioles are common in Nova Scotia during the summer months. Only the two listed below occur in numbers during the winter, although the Common Grackle and Red-winged Blackbird are observed occasionally.

COMMON STARLING
(Sturnus vulgaris)

Description
- smaller than a robin, beak long and pointed
- black, speckled with white, purple, blue and green
- in flight shows short square tail and pointed wings

Habitat
- near human habitation: cities, towns, villages, farms, bird feeders

Notes
- The Starling was introduced from Europe to New York in 1890 and has now spread throughout North America. It arrived in Nova Scotia about 1915 and is now present in huge flocks. In summer, it feeds mainly on insects and some fruit, especially cherries. In winter, starlings eat weed seeds, waste grain and frozen fruit.

BROWN-HEADED COWBIRD
(Molothrus ater)

Description
- smaller than a robin, beak short and conical
- male, black with brown head and neck
- female, brownish grey

Habitat
- ploughed fields, farm yards, pastures, bird feeders

Notes

Cowbirds gather in large flocks often in company with starlings and house sparrows. They feed on weed seeds, waste grain and fruit. Like many seed-eating birds, in summer they eat primarily insects. The Cowbird was not common in Nova Scotia 25 years ago, but its range has extended and it is now present in large numbers in farming areas. The Cowbird does not build a nest. Rather, it lays its eggs in the nests of other species of birds. The foster parents incubate and hatch the eggs and feed the young.

43

GROSBEAKS and FINCHES

Nine species of grosbeaks and finches occur regularly in Nova Scotia during the summer and most remain through the winter. In addition, the Cardinal is an occasional and colourful visitor to winter feeders.

EVENING GROSBEAK
(Hesperiphona vespertina)

Description
- a stout bird, slightly smaller than a robin, very heavy bill
- male: bright yellow, black tail, black and white wings
- female: olive-brown, yellowish along sides, black tail with white spots, black and white wings

Habitat
- everywhere, but more common in towns and villages.

Notes
- The Evening Grosbeak has recently extended its range into Nova Scotia from western Canada. Twenty years ago it visited Nova Scotia for only a few weeks each autumn and spring, but now is present throughout the winter, spring and much of the summer. It is a nomadic bird and small flocks apparently travel considerable distances in winter. It feeds on the seeds of maple and ash trees and is commonly found in orchards eating the frozen apples left on the trees. Evening Grosbeaks frequent bird feeders where sunflower seeds are provided.

PURPLE FINCH
(Carpodacus purpureus)

Description
- size of a sparrow
- male: rose-coloured, back striped with brown, brown wings and tail
- female: back grey striped with brown, breast white and heavily streaked with brown, white line above eye

Habitat
- open borders along woods, weeds and bushes in fields and orchards, shrubbery around homes

Notes
- In winter, the Purple Finch moves from the coniferous woods to the more open areas nearer human habitation. It feeds on weed seeds, dried fruit and berries, and commonly visits bird feeders where sunflower seeds are available.

45

PINE GROSBEAK
(Pinicola enucleator)

Description
- slightly smaller than a robin, heavy beak characteristic of grosbeaks
- male: generally rose-coloured, most intense on crown and rump; black wings and tail, 2 white wing bars
- female: generally grey, yellowish crown and rump, black wings and tail, 2 white wing bars

Habitat
- evergreen woods, orchards, shrubbery around homes

Notes
- The Pine Grosbeak is a winter visitor to Nova Scotia, and only a few remain through the summer. The number of these birds fluctuates from year to year, apparently depending upon the availability of food in the more northern forests. They travel in small flocks and feed on the seeds of conifer cones, maples and ashes, and on dried berries and other fruits.

46

REDPOLL
(Acanthis flammea)

Description
- size of small sparrow
- streaked brown, conspicuous red cap and black chin
- males develop a pink breast in late winter

Habitat
- open areas, fields, orchards, roadsides

Notes

The Redpoll is found in small flocks, frequently mixed with goldfinches. It usually feeds on seeds of weeds, alders, and birches. The number of these birds fluctuates and in some winters they are much more abundant than in others. They summer near the northern tree limits.

PINE SISKIN
(Spinus pinus)

Description
- size of small sparrow
- back olive-coloured, breast white, streaked all over with brown
- tail and wings dark, showing yellow especially during flight

Habitat
- feeding on weed seeds in fields and orchards, and on the seeds of spruce and pine in woodlands

Notes
- Pine Siskins occur in small flocks often mixed with goldfinches and redpolls. Their numbers fluctuate, being locally common in some years and uncommon in other winters. They are often found in gardens and may visit bird feeders. They usually nest in the deep coniferous forests.

AMERICAN GOLDFINCH
(Spinus tristis)

Description
- size of a sparrow
- generally yellowish, olive-brown back, dark tail and wings with white bars

Habitat
- open areas; feeding on clumps of weeds in fields, in shrubbery about gardens, or along roadsides

Notes
   - In summer the male Goldfinch is bright yellow with black wings and tail and is often called the Wild Canary. Watch the flight of these birds; it is characteristic and helps to identify them at a distance. It is a "roller-coaster" pattern, rising with the wing beats and gliding and falling between wing beats. Typically, they utter a distinctive twittering sound during the rising portion of this flight pattern.

WHITE-WINGED
CROSSBILL

RED
CROSSBILL

RED CROSSBILL
(Loxia curvirostra)

WHITE-WINGED CROSSBILL
(Loxia leucoptera)

The Red Crossbill and White-winged Crossbill show many similarities in plumage and habit and are described together.

Description
- size of a sparrow, bill crossed at tip
- male Red Crossbill: generally red, brighter on rump, brown wings and tail, no wing bars
- female Red Crossbill: generally olive-green, yellowish crown and rump, dark wings and tail, no wing bars
- White-winged Crossbills are similar to male and female Red Crossbills but have 2 conspicuous wing bars

Habitat
- usually coniferous woods, Red Crossbill also frequents towns and villages

Notes
- These are nomadic birds and wander in flocks over considerable distances. They may be fairly common one winter and not seen again for several years. Their wanderings are dependent upon the production of cones by the spruce and other coniferous trees. Crossbills are the only North American bird in which the mandibles forming the bills are crossed. This is an adaptation to pry cones apart and expose the seeds at the base of the scales. Crossbills, while feeding, may also take hold of the branches with their beaks and swing from twig to twig. In towns and orchards the Red Crossbill feeds on the seeds of deciduous trees, rose hips and frozen fruit.

SPARROWS and BUNTINGS

About 15 species of sparrows and buntings occur regularly in Nova Scotia, most during the summer months. Five are fairly common during the winter and are included in these *Nature Notes*. The House or English Sparrow is also included here for descriptive convenience, although it belongs to the weaver family and is not a true sparrow. All of these birds feed mainly on the ground.

DARK-EYED JUNCO
(Junco hyemalis)

Description
- the size of a sparrow
- upperparts slate-coloured, sometimes brownish, outer tail feathers white and most conspicuous during flight
- underparts: breast slate-coloured, abdomen white

Habitat
- open areas where there is an abundance of weeds

Notes
- The Junco is one of our most common winter birds and is often seen with sparrows and goldfinches on the ground eating weed seeds. They are frequent visitors to gardens and bird feeders. Juncos, in small flocks, usually visit several regular feeding sites each day. They often return to the same sites each winter. Juncos are present in Nova Scotia during summer but retreat more to the woodlands, where they are found on the ground and in low bushes searching for insects among the leaf litter.

TREE SPARROW
(Spizella arborea)

Description
- upperparts brown, chestnut-coloured cap, two white wing bars
- underparts unstreaked grey, single dark dot in centre of grey breast

Habitat
- weeds and shrubbery along roadsides and fields

Notes
- The Tree Sparrow is common in Nova Scotia only in winter. It summers in northern Quebec and Newfoundland. It is found in open areas and feeds exclusively on weed seeds. It may frequent bird feeders during the latter part of winter. It often travels in company with juncos, goldfinches, and various sparrows.

WHITE-THROATED SPARROW
(Zonotrichia albicollis)

Description
- upperparts brown, crown distinctly striped black and white, yellow spot in front of eye
- underparts grey, conspicuous white throat

Habitat
- in winter, among weeds and low bushes about cultivated fields and gardens

Notes
- Most White-throated Sparrows winter in the southern and central States but many remain in Nova Scotia. In summer, the White-throated Sparrow is found in the woodlands, often around clearings and cottages where its clear, flute-like song has made it one of our best known singers. It feeds on insects in summer and on weed seeds, especially those of goldenrod, in winter. It regularly visits winter bird feeders.

SONG SPARROW
(Melospiza melodia)

Description
- brown, back striped with black, breast white with black and brown streaks and a conspicuous central spot

Habitat
- generally uncommon in winter, may be locally common in sheltered sites
- shrubbery around homes and gardens, bushes along open streams and springs

Notes
- The Song Sparrow is a common Nova Scotian bird in summer when it frequents gardens, orchards, and thickets along the edges of woods and streams. Most winter in the southern States, but some remain in Nova Scotia in sheltered areas, preferably near water. The Song Sparrow feeds on insects, seeds, and wild fruit and may become a regular visitor to bird feeders.

SNOW BUNTING
(Plectrophenax nivalis)

Description
- a white bird, about the size of a large sparrow
- upperparts: back white with reddish-brown stripes; crown and rump reddish-brown; wings and tail white and black, most conspicuous when flying
- underparts: white, sides reddish-brown

Habitat
- open fields, especially dykelands and coastal regions

Notes
- The Snow Bunting, often called the Snow Bird, is common throughout the winter in fields where it feeds on weed seeds and waste grain. They are not found in wooded areas. Snow Buntings often mix with horned larks from which they can be distinguished by their lighter colour and by the white on the wings and tail. During winter, the edges of their feathers wear off and Snow Buntings gradually change from the brownish birds of early winter to the white and black birds of late winter and spring. They summer and nest in northern Quebec and the Arctic.

55

HOUSE SPARROW

HOUSE SPARROW
(Passer domesticus)

Description
- a large sparrow-like bird, generally greyish-brown
- male: grey crown, rump and tail; chestnut stripe back of eye, dark bib covering chin and breast
- female: more greyish than male, lacks bib

Habitat
- common in cities, towns and farmyards, seldom if ever occurs in woodlands or at a distance from human habitation.

Notes
- The House Sparrow, or English Sparrow, was introduced into North America from Europe, hopefully but unsuccessfully to control caterpillars. They were released in New York in 1851 and at other centres, including Nova Scotia, during the next 20 years. They have spread and are now common across North America. The young birds feed on insects, and the adults feed on seeds and wastes around human dwellings. This species does not migrate.

56

OTHER BIRDS TO LOOK FOR

A. Along the sea coast

Loons
- two species, Common Loon and Red-throated Loon
- both are large, slender, diving birds
- head and back grey, throat and underparts white
- Red-throated Loon: smaller, more lightly coloured, has slightly upcurved bill
- Common Loon: well known on summer lakes, along coast in winter
- markings of summer plumage, dark head and necklace of Common Loon and red throat of Red-throated Loon, are not present in winter plumage
- Common Loon runs for a considerable distance along the water when taking flight; Red-throated Loon rises directly into flight

Greater Scaup
- medium-sized duck
- male: head dark with greenish tinge, back grey, underparts white
- female: head and back brown, underparts white, characteristic white patch at base of bill
- both sexes during flight show white band along posterior border of wing
- gather in bays having rich supply of food, Atlantic and Northumberland coasts, lower Bay of Fundy
- collect into large rafts in late winter before northward migration

Bufflehead
- small, diving duck, about length of pigeon
- head large, back greenish or purplish, underparts white or grey
- male: characteristic white patch from eye to crown, white on wings
- female: cheek patch smaller than that of male, wing patch also smaller
- rises into flight directly without running along surface of water
- breeds in fresh water in western Canada
- found in small flocks in sheltered bays, along Atlantic and Northumberland coasts, Annapolis Basin

57

Oldsquaw
- diving duck, slightly smaller than a black duck
- male: head white with large brown cheek patch, throat and abdomen white with brown breast, back dark brown with white sides, wings brown, characteristic long pointed tail
- female: brown back, crown and breast; cheek patch smaller than male; tail less elongated
- breeds in Arctic
- along Atlantic and Northumberland coasts, Bay of Fundy, Minas Basin, and estuaries of larger rivers

Glaucous Gull
- large gull, about size of great black-backed gull
- wings and back light grey, no black
- along coast, especially in harbours and garbage dumps

Iceland Gull
- about size and colouration of herring gull, but no black wing tips
- along coast, especially in harbours and garbage dumps

Ring-bill Gull
- fairly common some winters, rare during others
- resembles herring gull in colouration including black wing tips, but is smaller and has characteristic black ring encircling bill
- immatures have black tail band
- along Atlantic and Northumberland coasts, lower Bay of Fundy and Annapolis Basin, showing a preference for harbours

Black-legged Kittiwake
- small gull, slightly larger than a pigeon
- white body and tail, grey wings, solid black wing tips, black legs
- tail squared or slightly forked, not rounded as in other gulls
- usually fly well out to sea, occasionally inshore and may be fairly numerous following a storm
- Atlantic and Northumberland coasts, lower Bay of Fundy
- watch for Kittiwakes when travelling on the Yarmouth, Digby, or P.E.I. ferries

Murres
- two species, Common Murre and Thick-billed Murre, with similar plumages
- both smaller than the black duck
- both with black upperparts and white underparts
- Common Murre has long, slender, black beak; sides of head white with black line back of eye
- Thick-billed Murre has shorter, thick, black beak; white cheeks with poorly defined black line behind eye

- both sit on rocks in erect position
- may collect into large rafts, usually well out to sea but seeking sheltered bays during storms
- often seen flying in groups, low over the water

Dovekie
- small sea-bird, about robin-sized
- black upperparts; white underparts including, in winter, throat and sides of head; small beak; no neck
- usually far out to sea, floating on surface, feeds on plankton
- seen inshore during storms and periods of rough seas when food is scarce
- may be found well inland during prolonged severe weather, often in a weak condition. These birds are stranded because Dovekies cannot take off from land and you can help launch them, if they are not too weak, by gently tossing them into the air.

B. Open Fresh Water, Fresh and Salt Water Marshes

Grebes
- two species winter in Nova Scotia, Red-necked Grebe and Horned Grebe
- both diving birds
- both, in winter, have a dark grey crown and back, light grey or white underparts
- Red-necked Grebe: medium-sized, long-necked, grey throat (red neck is seen in summer plumage only)
- Horned Grebe: small bird (smaller than a pigeon) with white throat
- open fresh water and streams, marshy ponds along coast, sometimes inshore coastal waters, Red-necked Grebe often common along Bay of Fundy

Canada Goose
- large bird, long neck, black head and neck showing characteristic white chin patch, greyish-brown back, light grey underparts
- "V-shaped" flocks in flight and "honking" voice are well known
- common during spring and fall migrations when they gather in large flocks on dykelands around the Minas Basin and upper Bay of Fundy
- most migrate south in winter, but large numbers winter on coastal marshes in Queen's, Shelburne, and Halifax counties

Purple Sandpiper
- robin-sized, the only shorebird regularly wintering in Nova Scotia
-upperparts striped dark brown with purplish tinge
- underparts white, breast striped with grey

- legs and base of bill yellow, long bill typical of waders
- occurs singly or in small flocks, rocky and sandy coasts, sandflats around Minas Basin and Northumberland shore, estuaries of larger rivers, among seaweeds on rocks of Bay of Fundy coast

Common Snipe
- about robin-sized, long bill
- head and back striped with brown, throat grey striped with brown, abdomen white, tail reddish and best seen in flight
- common summer bird, wet meadows and bogs
- less common in winter, around swamps and springs with open water

Short-eared Owl
- medium-sized owl
- brown streaked with greys and darker browns, lighter underneath
- wing span about one metre, slow wing beats
- seen at dusk and on cloudy days, flying near ground over meadows, dykelands, and coastal marshes

C. About Towns, Farms, and Open Country

Marsh Hawk
- male: bluish grey head and back, underparts white streaked with red-brown
- female: upperparts reddish-brown, underparts white streaked with red-brown
- both sexes have white rump — good identifying characteristic
- common in summer, sailing close to ground
- a few present in winter, over marshlands and dykelands surrounding the Minas Basin and upper Bay of Fundy

Saw-whet Owl
- about length of robin, smallest owl in Nova Scotia
- brown mottled with white, cinnamon on back, lighter underneath
- common in Nova Scotia but seldom seen because it lives in deep woods and hunts only at night
- in winter, during periods of cold and food shortages, they appear about farms and in villages, usually in a weakened condition; feed small bits of meat or strained baby food meat

Mockingbird
- about robin-sized
- upperparts including wings and tail dark grey, underparts light grey, white wing patches, outer tail feathers white and most conspicuous when flying
- a number reported in Nova Scotia each winter, primarily

during early winter
- in bushes, trees, and bird feeders feeding on fruit and berries; hedges of multiflora rose are frequented, feeding on rose hips

Waxwings
- two species: Cedar Waxwing, Bohemian Waxwing
- both smaller than robins
- Cedar Waxwing: yellowish-brown with crested head; black chin and forehead and extending back through eyes; wings greyish, often with red "wax" spots; tail greyish with terminal yellow bar
- common in summer feeding on berries and insects, irregular and rare winter visitor
- Bohemian Waxwing: similar to Cedar Waxwing but larger, more blue markings on wings
- nomadic birds, a number of small flocks are seen in Nova Scotia each winter
- feeds on berries

Northern Shrike
- about robin-sized
- underparts white, upperparts grey, wings and tail black with white wing patches and white outer tail feathers, black line through eye, bill hooked
- regular but uncommon winter visitor
- feeds on small birds and mice
- perches in high places such as tops of trees

Cardinal
- about robin-sized
- male Cardinal is red
- female Cardinal is brownish with red tinge; crest, bill and feet red
- uncommon winter visitor, several seen each winter often at bird feeders

Yellow-breasted Chat
- smaller than a robin
- upperparts olive-green, underparts bright yellow, black line through eye
- uncommon winter visitor, several seen each winter, usually during early winter, often about homes and garden shrubbery
- our largest member of the warbler family

WINTER BIRD
FEEDERS

Feeding birds is a pleasant and enjoyable hobby. It is a good way to learn to recognize species and to learn something about their habits. It helps birds through periods when food is scarce, especially during storms and icy rains. The birds will return the favour by supplementing their diet with weed seeds from your garden and by searching through your shrubs and trees for hibernating insects and insect eggs.

A number of birds can be attracted to a winter feeder on a regular basis. Depending on locality, these include: Sharp-shinned Hawk, Common Pheasant, Rock Dove, Mourning Dove, Hairy Woodpecker, Downy Woodpecker, Blue Jay, Grey Jay, Common Raven, Common Crow, Black-capped Chickadee, White-breasted Nuthatch, Red-breasted Nuthatch, Starling, Robin, House Sparrow, Common Grackle, Brown-headed Cowbird, Evening Grosbeak, Purple Finch, Common Redpoll, Pine Siskin, American Goldfinch, Dark-eyed Junco, Tree Sparrow, White-throated Sparrow, Song Sparrow, Snow Bunting. Other species may occasionally come to a feeder, and a rare visit by a Mockingbird, Waxwing, or Cardinal is an exciting pleasure.

A simple shelf is adequate, fastened to a window sill, tree or post. A feeder with two sides and a roof is better since it provides shelter for the birds and prevents the food from blowing away. If possible, the feeder should be placed near shrubbery. Shelter for escape from Sharp-shinned Hawks, cats, and dogs, is important for the smaller birds.

A greater variety of birds will be attracted if the bird seed is supplemented with some of the following foods:

Suet — fasten to tree in a net, or make a suet log by cutting holes in a log and packing them with suet.
    — for birds that usually eat insects: Hairy and Downy Woodpeckers, Nuthatches, Blue Jays, Black-capped Chickadees, Starlings, Crows, etc.

Sunflower Seeds — a must for Evening Grosbeaks
    - also eaten by Chickadees, Blue Jays, Nuthatches

Chicken Scratch — available at agricultural feed stores
    - seed-eating birds: Pheasants, Sparrows, Finches, Juncos, Blue Jays

Corn - cracked corn available at agricultural feed stores
    - Pheasants, Sparrows, Finches, Juncos, Blue Jays

- hang a dried ear of corn from a branch and watch the antics of Blue Jays feeding on it.

Raisins, Dried Berries, Sliced Apples, etc. — Robins

Egg Yolk, hard-boiled — insect eating birds: Chickadees, Nuthatches, Woodpeckers

Margarine - a favourite of Chickadees

Water - while it is not possible to keep water available on cold days, birds will appreciate a drink when it can be provided.

CHECK LIST OF WINTER BIRDS

The following list includes those birds that occur regularly in Nova Scotia during the winter period. Some species are commonly observed throughout the province, others are fairly numerous in certain localities only and are usually not found elsewhere, and others are scarce but will be seen a few times during most winters. The list does not include rare and occasional visitors. It is based on the "Annotated List of Nova Scotia Birds" by Robie W. Tufts, and "Nova Scotia Birds" by L.B. Macpherson and C.R. Allen, both published by the Nova Scotia Museum in Halifax.

Species	Date First Observed	Location First Observed
Common Loon		
Red-throated Loon		
Red-necked Grebe		
Horned Grebe		
Canada Goose		
Mallard		
Black Duck		
Greater Scaup		
Common Goldeneye		
Bufflehead		
Oldsquaw		
Common Eider		
King Eider		
White-winged Scoter		
Common Merganser		
Red-breasted Merganser		
Goshawk		
Sharp-shinned Hawk		
Red-tailed Hawk		
Rough-legged Hawk		
Bald Eagle		
Marsh Hawk		
Spruce Grouse		
Ruffed Grouse		

Species	Date First Observed	Location First Observed
Common Pheasant		
Grey Partridge		
Common Snipe		
Purple Sandpiper		
Glaucous Gull		
Iceland Gull		
Great Black-backed Gull		
Herring Gull		
Ring-billed Gull		
Black-headed Gull		
Black-legged Kittiwake		
Razorbill		
Common Murre		
Thick-billed Murre		
Dovekie		
Black Guillemot		
Common Puffin		
Rock Dove		
Mourning Dove		
Great Horned Owl		
Snowy Owl		
Barred Owl		
Short-eared Owl		
Saw-whet Owl		
Pileated Woodpecker		
Hairy Woodpecker		
Downy Woodpecker		
Black-backed Three-toed Woodpecker		
Horned Lark		
Grey Jay		
Blue Jay		
Common Raven		

66

Species	Date First Observed	Location First Observed
Common Crow		
Black-capped Chickadee		
Boreal Chickadee		
White-breasted Nuthatch		
Red-breasted Nuthatch		
Brown Creeper		
Mockingbird		
Robin		
Golden-crowned Kinglet		
Bohemian Waxwing		
Cedar Waxwing		
Northern Shrike		
Starling		
Yellow-rumped Warbler		
Yellow-breasted Chat		
House Sparrow		
Common Grackle		
Red-winged Blackbird		
Brown-headed Cowbird		
Cardinal		
Evening Grosbeak		
Purple Finch		
Pine Grosbeak		
Common Redpoll		
Pine Siskin		
American Goldfinch		
Red Crossbill		
White-winged Crossbill		
Vesper Sparrow		
Dark-eyed Junco		
Tree Sparrow		
White-throated Sparrow		

Species	Date First Observed	Location First Observed
Song Sparrow		
Lapland Longspur		
Snow Bunting		

MAMMALS

About 45 species of mammals are found in Nova Scotia, excluding the seals and whales. Many mammals are nocturnal but may be seen during the early morning, at dusk, and on cloudy days. Other mammals may be seen in the appropriate habitats at any time of the day.

A number of Nova Scotian mammals hibernate and usually will not be seen during the winter. Thus, such well-known mammals as the black bear, bats, jumping mice, and chipmunks are not included in *Nature Notes* because they usually remain in hibernation until spring. Other hibernators, such as the skunk and woodchuck, are included because they often leave hibernation in mid-February and may be seen during the end of winter.

This section also includes a "Quick Guide" that groups the mammals on the basis of size and overall colour. It is intended to help the beginner by limiting his search to only a few possible species. It groups only those mammals that are included in *Nature Notes*. Always read the descriptions and remember that there are other mammals in Nova Scotia that are not listed in this "Guide". You may find these less common mammals and you will need a more complete "Field Guide" to identify them.

Originally, *Nature Notes* was to be co-authored by a friend, Dr. Austin Cameron, author of a number of research reports and publications on Canadian mammals. Dr. Cameron died while the manscrupt was still at an early stage of preparation. However, he prepared the preliminary notes on many of the mammals included in this section and his contribution is acknowledged with appreciation.

QUICK GUIDE TO THE MAMMALS

	Mammal or Group	Page
A. - **Less than 15 cm head-body length, tail not included (mouse size)**		
- mostly brown or grey, lighter underparts, nose pointed, tiny ears and eyes	Long-tailed Shrew Short-tailed Shrew	72 73
- mostly black or dark brown, lighter underparts, large fore-feet, tentacles around nose	Star-nosed Mole	74
- mostly grey or brown, white underparts, large ears, long tail	Deer Mouse White-footed Mouse	81 81
- mostly grey or brown, long tail	House Mouse	86
- mostly reddish-brown or grey, lighter underparts, ears small, tail short	Red-backed Vole Meadow Vole	82 84
B. - **15 to 25 cm head-body length, tail not included (squirrel size)**		
- mostly white, tail tip and eyes black, ears short	Short-tailed Weasel	90
- mostly brown, grey underparts, tail long and scaly	Brown Rat	85
- mostly reddish-brown, white underparts, tail long and bushy	Red Squirrel	78
- mostly light brown, white underparts, tail long and bushy, web connects wrist and ankles	Flying Squirrel	79
C. - **30 to 50 cm head-body length, tail not included (domestic cat size)**		
- black or dark brown, body slender	Mink	91
- brown, light brown or grey underparts, tail scaly and flattened fron side to side	Muskrat	83

70

	Mammal or Group	Page
- black, 2 white stripes along back	Skunk	92
- white, long ears, large hind feet, short tail	Snowshoe Hare	76
- dark grey, reddish tinge, black feet, broad head, short bushy tail	Woodchuck	77
D. - **50 cm to 1 m head-body length, tail not included (dog size)**		
- brown, tail long and tapering	Otter	93
- dark brown, tail flat and trowel-like	Beaver	80
- reddish, white underparts, long bushy tail with white tip	Red Fox	88
- dark brown, numerous sharp quills	Porcupine	87
- mostly grey, brown sprinkles, short tail, conspicuous tufts on ears and ruffs hanging from cheeks	Lynx	94
- mostly brown, spotted, short tail, ear tufts and cheek ruffs absent or not conspicuous	Bobcat	95
- mostly brown, black mask, tail bushy and ringed	Raccoon	89
E. - **Head-body length more than 1 m**		
- size of domestic calf, greyish-brown, long legs, underside of tail white	White-tailed Deer	97
- size of domestic cow, dark brown, long legs, short tail, "bell" of long hair under throat	Moose	99

SHREWS and MOLES

The shrews and moles belong to the order of mammals known as Insectivores. They are small, mouse-like animals with a long snout and short legs. They tunnel through the soil or beneath the leaf litter and, as their order name suggests, feed primarily on insects and other small invertebrates. Eight species of shrews and moles occur in Nova Scotia. The following are the ones most frequently observed.

LONG-TAILED SHREWS
(Sorex, several species)

Description
- size of house mouse or smaller, medium brown above, pale brown below
- pointed nose, ears and eyes tiny, velvety fur
- tail 1/3 or more of total length

Habitat
- some species common throughout province, other species rare
- wooded areas, usually deciduous or mixed woods
- some species near water, or in damp soil

Notes
- Six species of Long-tailed Shrews occur in Nova Scotia, but they are difficult to distinguish in the wild. Although several species are common, they are seldom seen. Domestic cats frequently kill Shrews but rarely eat them, because they have a disagreeable odour. They live in tunnels in the ground and burrow beneath the snow and leaf litter. When on the surface, their movements are quick and "nervous". They feed primarily on insects and other invertebrates. One species, the water shrew, swims readily under water. Another species, the pigmy shrew, is the smallest mammal in North America.

72

SHORT-TAILED SHREW
(Blarina brevicauda)

Description
- about the size of house mouse, grey-black in colour
- pointed nose; ears and eyes tiny; short, velvety fur
- tail short, less than ¼ of total length

Habitat
- very common throughout province
- moist hardwoods, mixed woodlands, wet areas
- sometimes invading fields and meadows

Notes
- The Short-tailed Shrew is one of our most common small mammals although it is seldom seen. It can be distinguished from a mouse by its short fur and pointed snout, and from moles by the front feet which are smaller than the hind feet. It burrows through loose soil, leaf litter and snow, and is frequently found in the runways of other small mammals. It feeds on insects and other small invertebrates, as well as on long-tailed shrews and mice. One of its salivary glands secretes a poison similar to that found in poisonous snakes, and its bite is sufficient to kill a mouse and to cause pains in humans. The Short-tailed Shrew is often caught by cats but seldom eaten.

STAR-NOSED MOLE
(Condylura cristata)

Description
- size of mouse, total length 16 to 20 cm, tail about 1/3 total length
- upperparts black or dark brown, underparts grey
- front feet broad and shovel-like, no external ears
- end of nose surrounded by 22 finger-like tentacles ("starnosed")
- tail long, thick, scaly, constricted at base

Habitat
- common throughout Nova Scotia, wet habitats
- swamps, meadows, marshes, lake and stream banks

Notes
- The Star-nosed Mole tunnels through the moist soil a few centimeters below the surface. In doing so, it strokes the earth aside with its shovel-like fore-feet. When burrowing deeply, it pushes the earth out onto the surface, forming "mole hills". Its paddle-like feet and large tail make it an excellent swimmer. It swims long distances under water and occasionally may be seen swimming under the ice. In winter, it tunnels under the snow and frequently is seen on the surface. The nose tentacles are highly developed touch receptors, partly compensating for its poor eyesight. The Star-nosed Mole feeds on a variety of insects, worms, and aquatic invertebrates.

74

HARES and RABBITS

Hares and rabbits are in some ways similar to rodents. Both groups are herbivorous and have chisel-like incisor teeth. However, hares and rabbits differ in that they have long hind legs and feet which are adapted for jumping, long ears and a short tail. Of the several species of hares and rabbits in North America, only the snowshoe hare is native to Nova Scotia.

SNOWSHOE HARE

SNOWSHOE HARE
(Lepus americanus)

Description
-size of domestic cat; head-body length 45 cm, tail 3 to 4 cm
-long ears, large hind feet
-coat white (brown in summer), tips of ears dusky
-confused only with domestic rabbit which is smaller and found
 near human settlements

Habitat
-common throughout Nova Scotia
-mixed or deciduous woodland, alder thickets, shrubby borders
 along farmlands

Notes
-In summer the Snowshoe Hare feeds on grasses and herbaceous
plants, and in winter subsists chiefly on the twigs and bark of trees
and shrubs. Twigs that have been browsed by hares have a ragged
appearance as this animal makes several "chomps" before severing
the twig. Twigs browsed by deer, on the other hand, have clean cuts
because the deer severs the twig in one bite. Hares are active mainly at
night or on cloudy days. As their name suggests, they have large feet
covered with dense hair and they are able to run along the top of the
snow. Snowshoe Hares show a population cycle, reaching a peak of
abundance every 8 to 10 years and then declining dramatically in
numbers, often by as much as 80%, between peaks. Their major
predators are lynxes, bobcats, foxes, and great-horned owls.

RODENTS

Rodents are the most numerous group of mammals and feed
primarily on plants. They are gnawing animals and chew with a side-
to-side, rather than up-and-down, movement of the jaw. Hard
enamel covers the front of the tooth and, as the softer dentine along
the back of the tooth wears off, forms a sharp chisel-like edge. These
incisor teeth are well developed and, unlike other mammals, continue
to grow throughout life to replace the ends worn by gnawing. About
18 species of rodents occur in Nova Scotia. The following are the ones
that are more frequently observed.

WOODCHUCK
(Marmota monax)

Description
- size of domestic cat; head-body length 40 cm, tail 10 cm; weight 2 to 4.5 kg
- large rodent, broad head, short ears, heavy body, short tail, short legs
- general coloration dark grey, may be some reddish-brown, shows considerable colour variations, feet and tail dark, face lighter

Habitat
- locally common, mainland Nova Scotia, open country
- bush lands, farmlands, hedgerows, often near streams

Notes

-Woodchucks, or Groundhogs, excavate underground burrows that may be 9 to 12 metres in length and have several entrances. The Woodchuck lives primarily on grasses and cultivated plants such as clover and alfalfa. It goes into hibernation early in October, often before the first frosts, and will not be seen during much of the winter. It emerges early in the spring, but never as early as "Ground Hog Day" on February 2, and may be seen about the end of February or during most of March.

RED SQUIRREL
(Tamiasciurus hudsonicus)

Description
-total length including tail about 30 cm
-upperparts bright reddish-brown, underparts dull white
-tail long, bushy, often bright orange-red in winter

Habitat
-common throughout Nova Scotia
-coniferous or mixed woodlands, prefers areas where the trees range 6 metres or more in height
-may visit winter feeding stations

Notes
-The Red Squirrel is one of our best known wild mammals. Unlike most mammals, it is active during the daylight hours and its loud chatter is a familiar sound in spruce and fir woodlands. It scampers up trees, over branches, and may leap several metres to the next tree. It feeds on seeds, nuts, and buds of all kinds. It harvests evergreen cones and buries them in damp soil to be dug up later when needed. The caches may contain more than a bushel of cones. The Red Squirrel also feeds on various mushrooms, even some species that are poisonous to man. It may live in a hollow in a tree, or under a rock or log pile. It is preyed upon by hawks, owls, weasels and bobcats.

NORTHERN FLYING SQUIRREL
(Glaucomys sabrinus)

Description
-size of red squirrel, about 30 cm including tail
-pale fawn coloured above, white underparts
-web connects the wrists and ankles
-tail flattened and bushy, eyes larger than other squirrels

Habitat
-throughout Nova Scotia, more common in south-western counties
-coniferous or mixed woodlands, prefers areas with tall evergreens

Notes
-The Northern Flying Squirrel appears at dusk and is active only at night. For this reason it is rarely seen although it is quite common. It sleeps in hollow trees during the day. Sometimes it takes up residence in attics of old houses and is the basis for many reports of "haunted" houses. It cannot actually fly but it can glide distances of up to 45 metres, using its tail as a rudder. The Flying Squirrel feeds on nuts, seeds, and berries, as well as insects and small birds and mammals. The Flying Squirrel makes a charming pet for people who stay up until the early morning hours.

BEAVER
(Castor canadensis)

Description
- large, stout rodent; head-body length 50 to 75 cm, tail 30 to 50 cm; weighs up to about 30 kg
- general colouration dark brown, short blunt head, webbed hind feet
- tail flattened and paddle-like

Habitat
- common throughout Nova Scotia
- along streams and margins of lakes

Notes
-The Beaver feeds on the bark of such hardwood trees as poplar (its favourite), birch, willow, and sometimes alder if other food is scarce. The Beaver fells the trees and cuts them into chunks that can be more easily handled. The Beaver home is constructed of sticks and is dome-shaped (the lodge of the muskrat is built of herbaceous plants such as cattail and is much smaller). Beavers often build a dam across a stream to ensure a pond 2 or 3 metres in depth. The branches of trees are stored in the mud in this artificial pond and the Beavers emerge from their lodges, under the ice, to feed on them. Beavers, therefore, may not be in evidence in mid-winter although Beaver lodges and Beaver ponds may be found. Lodges that are occupied may be identified in winter because the snow melts around the opening of the ventilation shaft at the top of the lodge. When the water is not frozen, the Beaver slaps its flat tail on the water when alarmed before submerging.

DEER MOUSE

DEER MOUSE
(Peromyscus maniculatus)

WHITE-FOOTED MOUSE
(Peromyscus leucopus)

The Deer and White-footed Mice are closely related species, are similar in appearance and cannot easily be distinguished in the field. The following notes apply to both species.

Description
- total length 17 to 20 cm, including tail
- upperparts cinnamon with a yellowish wash, sometimes greyish
- underparts white, suffused with a soft grey in young
- cinnamon or grey of back clearly demarcated from white underparts
- ears and eyes large (Mickey Mouse)
- tail at least 1/3 of total length, also grey above and white below

Habitat
- Deer Mouse common throughout Nova Scotia
- White-footed Mouse in western counties only
- dry habitats, deciduous or mixed woodlands, brush piles, woodland cabins

Notes
- The Deer and White-footed Mice are among our most abundant wild mice. They are nocturnal and will usually be seen at dusk, but their tracks will often be seen in the snow. They live mostly on the ground but climb trees readily. They are harmless and make amusing pets. They feed on seeds and insects and store seeds in holes in trees and logs. They can be nuisances if they invade summer cottages where they often build nests in matresses. Their predators include owls, hawks, cats, foxes, weasels, and short-tailed shrews.

RED-BACKED VOLE
(Clethrionomys gapperi)

Description
- total length, including tail, 10 to 15 cm
- upperparts reddish-brown, underparts yellowish
- body plump; tail short, about 1/3 of head-body length
- ears short, almost hidden in fur
- a dark colour phase comprises about 10% of population: back is dark sooty-grey, almost black, belly is medium grey
- blunt nose and "loose", reddish hair fur distinguish Red-backed Vole from Short-tailed Shrew

Habitat
- common throughout Nova Scotia woodlands
- evergreen or mixed woods having plenty of leaf mold, rotting stumps, and brush piles

Notes
- The Red-backed Vole, or Red-backed Mouse, is one of the most common mammals on the forest floor, a habitat it often shares with deer mice. It burrows under the leaf litter and often takes shelter under brush piles. It is rarely found in open, grassy areas where the meadow vole occurs. In winter, it feeds on buds, nuts, seeds, tubers, and bark. It is hunted by hawks and owls, and several mammals such as weasels, mink, and foxes.

MUSKRAT
(Ondatra zibethicus)

Description
- size of a small house cat; head-body length 30 cm, tail 25 to 30 cm; weight 1 to 2 kg
- upperparts brown, underparts pale brown, chin dirty white
- hind feet partly webbed; tail hairless, scaly, flattened from side to side
- may be confused with first year beaver which, however, has a paddle-like tail and blunter head

Habitat
- common throughout Nova Scotia
- lake margins, ponds, streams, bogs, reed and cattail marshes

Notes
- The Muskrat is a semi-aquatic animal, living in or near water and feeding on the leaves, stems, and roots of water plants. It is mainly nocturnal and will usually be seen in the early morning or evening or on cloudy days. It builds a lodge, or nest, of herbaceous plants, usually cattail, which is dome-shaped and may be more than 1 m in height (the beaver's lodge is built of sticks). The entrance to the lodge is underwater and, once the ponds and lakes are frozen, muskrats are seldom seen although their lodges are much in evidence. Along rivers and streams, the muskrat may build its home by tunnelling into the bank. Muskrats disperse during the spring and fall, and they may travel considerable distances across land looking for new locations in which to build a home. Road kills are frequently seen at these times. Mink, foxes, otters, hawks, and owls prey on this mammal.

MEADOW VOLE
(Microtus pennsylvanicus)

Description
- total length, including tail, up to 17 cm
- upperparts dull yellowish-brown or greyish-brown (never
- reddish-brown or sooty grey as Red-backed Vole)
- underparts white
- tail short, less than 1/3 head-body length; legs short
- ears small, almost hidden in fur
- fur long and "loose" giving animal a "dishevelled" look

Habitat
- common throughout Nova Scotia
- open fields and meadows, rarely woodlands (except on some
small islands along the coast where the forested areas are not
occupied by Red-backed Vole).

Notes
- Almost everyone has seen the Meadow Vole, or Meadow
Mouse, or at least has seen its runways meandering through fields
and overgrown pastures. It is most active during the early morning
and the evening. In winter it feeds primarily on grass under the snow
and on seeds and roots. Approximately every four years it reaches a
peak of abundance and when it does it often inflicts serious injury on
small fruit trees by girdling them. It is hunted by a large number of
predators such as red-tailed and rough-legged hawks, owls, foxes,
and weasels.

BROWN (NORWAY) RAT
(Rattus norvegicus)

Description
- about the size of a squirrel; head-body length 15 to 23 cm, tail 15 to 23 cm
- coat is dull brown above, greyish or light yellowish below
- tail long and scaly

Habitat
- near or in human habitation, farm buildings, garbage dumps, etc.

Notes
- The Brown Rat was originally native to central Asia but has followed man to almost every part of the world. It is generally found near human habitation, eats almost everything, and is a nuisance. When the first settlers came to eastern North America they also brought the black rat with them, but this species has been replaced by the Brown Rat and is no longer found in the Atlantic Provinces.

HOUSE MOUSE
(Mus musculus)

Description
- total length, including tail, 16 to 20 cm
- upperparts brownish-grey, underparts medium grey or brownish-grey
- no clear line of demarcation between colour of back and belly
- tail almost as long as head-body length, short-haired, scaly
- ears long

Habitat
- common throughout Nova Scotia
- in and around human dwellings, adjacent crop land, farm buildings

Notes
- The House Mouse is a native of southern Asia and was brought to North America from Europe. It is a nuisance for it lives in human dwellings, eats almost anything, and breeds continuously throughout the year. It is most frequently controlled by trapping.

PORCUPINE
(Erethizon dorsatum)

Description
- dog-sized; large, stout rodent with small head and short tail
- head-body length 47 to 70 cm, tail 15 to 30 cm, weighs 2.5 to 7.5 kg or more
- body covered with thick, black hair and numerous sharp, barbed quills
- walks on soles of the feet so its track resembles that of a small bear

Habitat
- common throughout mainland Nova Scotia, rare in Cape Breton
- evergreen and mixed woodlands

Notes
- The Porcupine is a vegetarian and in winter prefers the inside bark of trees, which it obtains by chewing away the outer bark. It does considerable damage to trees. Porcupines have few enemies because of their arsenal of quills. The quills are barbed and, if they should penetrate the flesh of another animal, are inclined to work their way in more deeply with the movement of the victim's skin muscles. Contrary to popular opinion, the porcupine cannot throw its quills but it can thrash its tail so rapidly that it easy to imagine that the quills are thrown. Porcupines like salt and have chewed many camp tables and perspiration-coated axe handles. Salt probably also attracts Porcupines to highways, and this may partially explain the large number of road-kills seen in wooded regions.

CARNIVORES

The carnivores include a number of mammals that feed primarily on meat and fish, although many also eat vegetable matter. The teeth of carnivores are characteristic. The canines are long and curved inward for tearing, and the premolars of most carnivores are flattened and knife-like for cutting. Twelve species of carnivores occur in Nova Scotia and eight of these are included in *Nature Notes*. The black bear hibernates and will not be seen during the winter.

RED FOX
(Vulpes vulpes)

Description
- size of a small dog; head-body length 60 cm, tail 40 cm; weighs from 3 to 6 kg
- body usually reddish, underparts white, lustrous fur, black legs and feet, pointed ears
- tail long, dark, bushy, white-tipped

Habitat
- common throughout Nova Scotia
- open woodlands, brush borders of fields and pastures, dykelands

Notes
- The Red Fox is well known to anyone who lives in rural areas. Its food consists of fruit, berries, insects, mice, ground-nesting birds, grouse, and even hares. It digs a den, which usually has several entrances, or enlarges burrows dug by other animals. Foxes are nocturnal hunters and will be most commonly seen in the early morning or the latter part of the afternoon. When hunting, they may range 6 to 8 km from their den. Two additional colour phases occur: the "cross fox" has a dark patch or cross on the back between the shoulders, and the "silver fox" which is black with a few white-tipped hairs scattered throughout the fur on the back. All colour phases belong to the same species and may even occur in the same litter.

88

RACCOON
(Procyon lotor)

Description
- size of a small dog, head-body length 50 to 70 cm, tail 20 to 25 cm, weighs up to 12 kg
- general colour buffy brown, individuals ranging from dark to light, black mask over eyes, tail bushy with black rings

Habitat
- common throughout mainland Nova Scotia, locally common in Cape Breton
- wooded areas, except dense conifers, preferably near water

Notes
- The Raccoon is the only mammal in Nova Scotia with a black mask and a ringed tail. It is nocturnal and will usually be seen at dusk. It becomes inactive during cold weather, but will be active in February and March. Its den is usually in a hollow tree or excavated under rocks. Raccoons are intelligent and playful animals. They are well known about woodland cottages and houses in rural areas where they scavenge through the garbage for food. Raccoons feed on fruit, vegetables (especially corn), frogs, aquatic animals, mice, and birds' eggs.

SHORT-TAILED WEASEL
(Mustela erminea)

Description
- male size of squirrel; head-body length 20 cm, tail 9 cm; female 1/3 smaller
- body long and slender, pure white in winter, legs short, eyes and tip of tail black

Habitat
- ground dweller, common throughout Nova Scotia
- open woods, hedgerows, sandy beaches, farm buildings

Notes
-The Short-tailed Weasel, or Ermine, is usually seen running swiftly under and over logs and rocks. In winter only the black eyes and the black tip on the tail can be clearly seen against the snow. The Weasel is brown with a white abdomen during the summer. It preys on mice, birds, and almost any small creature it can capture. It sometimes kills grouse and domestic poultry by seizing the bird by the neck and severing the jugular vein. The weasel's curiosity and fearlessness will often reward the patient observer with several darting appearances.

90

MINK
(Mustela vison)

Description
-male: size of a small house cat, head-body length 35 to 40 cm, tail 18 cm, weight 1.7 to 2.3 kg; female 1/3 smaller
-body long and slender, black or dark brown, chin often white; legs short; tail bushy, about 1/3 total length

Habitat
-common throughout Nova Scotia
-along rivers, streams, lakes and tidal areas; rarely far from water
-wooded and dykeland areas

Notes
-The Mink resembles a large, black ermine, to which it is related. It lives in a den in the river bank or under a stump. The mink is an excellent swimmer. It feeds on frogs, fish, and other aquatic animals, as well as on mice, muskrats, and other small mammals and occasionally birds. In turn, it is hunted by hawks, owls, foxes, lynx, and bobcats. Various domestic varieties ranging in colour from pale grey to dark brown have been developed.

91

STRIPED SKUNK
(Mephitis mephitis)

Description
   -size of small house cat; head-body length 35 cm, tail 23 cm
   -body black, two white stripes along back
   -tail bushy, often elevated when walking

Habitat
   -fairly common in northern and eastern Nova Scotia
   -open country, not deep woods, young growth, shrubby borders
   of farmlands

Notes
   -During the 1920's and 1930's, disease killed most of the skunks
in Nova Scotia. They are now spreading through Nova Scotia again
and are most common along the New Brunswick border, north shore,
and eastern counties. They have reached the eastern Annapolis
Valley but are not, as yet, present in the western counties or Cape
Breton. The Skunk lives in a den in the ground, under barns, or in
abandoned buildings. It is often quite fearless and can be closely
approached. A pair of glands at the base of the tail produce a fluid
which has a strong, musky odour. When alarmed, the Skunk can
spray this fluid several metres. The scent is very unpleasant and the
spray can cause severe irritation and temporary blindness if it should
get into the eyes. Skunks feed on insects, small rodents, birds' eggs
and a variety of wild fruits. It has a winter sleep but is not a true
hibernator and may emerge (usually the male) in mid-winter if the
weather is mild.

OTTER
(Lutra canadensis)

Description
-size of small dog; head-body length 75 cm, tail 40 cm, female smaller; weighs 4 to 10 kg.
-body slender, medium brown, shiny; legs short, head round, tail long and tapering, hind feet webbed

Habitat
-throughout Nova Scotia, common around Bras d'Or Lake
-along larger streams and lakes, sometimes entering ocean

Notes
-The Otter spends much of its time in water pursuing fish and other aquatic animals, on which it feeds. It is about the size of a beaver and is often mistaken for one while swimming. Its tapering tail distinguishes it from the beaver. The Otter can swim considerable distances under water. Its den is excavated in a bank along a river or lake. The Otter makes snow slides or mud slides and it frolics in a playful manner. Its legs are short and it ploughs a deep furrow through the snow.

93

LYNX
(Lynx lynx)

Description
- short-tailed cat, size of medium-sized dog
- head-body length 80 cm, tail 12 cm, weight about 7 to 14 kg
- light-grey in colour with sprinkling of pale brown, no spotting
- conspicuous "pencils" or long black tufts on the tips of ears
- feet yellowish and disproportionately large
- conspicuous "ruffs" hang from cheeks
- can be confused only with the Bobcat (see next species)

Habitat
- common locally in Cape Breton highlands, rare elsewhere
- deep coniferous or mixed woods, usually far from civilization

Notes
- The Lynx feeds chiefly on snowshoe hares. When hares are at a low in their population cycle, the Lynx is often hard-pressed for food and will sometimes wander into farmlands or approach human settlements. Although not uncommon in some areas, it is rarely seen since it is secretive and nocturnal. Its tracks are seldom seen in damp mud because, like all cats, it does not like to get its feet wet. When the track is seen it is often mistaken for that of a much larger cat because of its disproportionately large feet. The lynx has been declining in numbers in Nova Scotia since the early 1970's, perhaps because of competition with the more versatile bobcat.

BOBCAT
(Lynx rufus)

Description
- short-tailed cat, size of medium-sized dog
- head-body length 65 to 70 cm, tail 14 cm, weight about 7 to 14 kg
- yellowish-brown in colour, considerable spotting especially on legs
- ear tufts absent or very short, neck ruff scanty, feet not disproportionately large

Habitat
- open woodlands, wet bushy area, sometimes near civilization

Notes
- The Bobcat, or Nova Scotia Wildcat, can be confused with the lynx. The Bobcat, however, does not have conspicuous ear tufts, a neck ruff, or disproportionately large feet. If it is possible to examine a specimen closely, note that only the upper surface of the tail tip is black in the Bobcat, and the tail usually has a few dark bars. The black surrounds the tail tip of the lynx and there is no barring. Throughout most of North America, the Bobcat is about 25% smaller than the lynx, but those occuring in the Maritime Provinces are large and may weigh as much as a lynx. The Bobcat feeds on a variety of small mammals and birds and is not so dependent upon a single prey species as is the lynx. Although it may be locally common, it is secretive and not often seen. Its track is similar to that of the domestic cat, but is almost twice the size. The Bobcat has increased in numbers in Nova Scotia since 1970. It dens in a hollow log or tree.

WHITE-TAIL DEER

DEER and MOOSE

The deer and moose belong to the order of mammals known as the Artiodactyla ("even toes") in which the 3rd and 4th toes are the same size, covered with horn (nail material), and form much of the foot. The other toes are small or absent. Domestic cattle, sheep, pigs, etc. also belong to this group.

WHITE-TAILED DEER
(Odocoileus virginianus)

Description
- about size of calf; head-body length 1.7 to 1.8 m, tail 15 to 25 cm; height at shoulder about 1m; average weight of male 90 kg, up to 135 kg; females smaller
- legs long, hooves cleft like those of domestic sheep but more pointed
- winter coat greyish-brown above (summer coat is more reddish), white underparts
- antler is distinctive having one main beam from which one to five sharp-pointed spikes project upward, carried by males only, shed annually during winter
- underside of tail white, this white flag is upright and conspicuous as deer bounds through woods and fields

Habitat
- common in wooded areas throughout Nova Scotia
- woodland cuttings and burns with young growth; open margins of woods, near fields and orchards

Notes
- Unlike the moose, the White-tailed Deer shuns mature forests; it prefers more open areas where there are small trees and shrubs on which it can browse during the winter months. In summer deer feed on grasses and herbaceous plants. In winters when there are heavy snows, deer form "yards" where a herd of up to 20 or 25 animals will stay together until spring. Usually "yards" are located in groves of evergreen trees, often in swamps near hardwoods where the deer can obtain food. The antlers are formed of bone and are quite different from the horns of cattle. They grow quickly and are covered by a thin skin, or "velvet", which is well supplied with blood vessels. When fully formed, in October, the velvet dries and is rubbed off against trees to expose the well polished antlers. The antlers are usually shed between December and February, the younger animals holding their antlers longest.

MOOSE

MOOSE
(Alces alces)

Description
- size of domestic cow, total length 1.9 to 2.6 m, stands 2 m at shoulder
- adults dark brown; young reddish-brown, lack spots
- long snout; long, gangly legs; "bell" of long hair under throat
- head and shoulders large, rump small
- bull moose grows antlers each year, shed in late fall or during the winter

Habitat
- found throughout Nova Scotia; larger numbers in the five northern and eastern counties, in Cape Breton Highlands, and in the general Tobeatic region
- forested areas, near swamps, ponds and lakes

Notes

- The Moose is a wilderness animal and, unlike deer, soon disappears when civilization invades its domain. In summer much of its time is spent wading about in shallow ponds and lakes feeding on various types of aquatic vegetation. In winter, it moves to the uplands and subsists on the twigs of such hardwoods as cherry, willow, birch, and maple, as well as fir and yew. When the snow is deep, several moose band together and pack the snow down to form a moose "yard". Unlike deer, which move quietly, moose often make a great deal of noise travelling through the underbrush. Adult bull moose weigh on the average about 450 kg, but are reported to exceed 600 kg. The bull moose is considered to be one of the most dangerous wild animals during the breeding season in the fall, and the female can be even more dangerous when protecting her young in early summer. The antlers, like those of the deer described above, are formed of bone and may measure up to 2 m across. The calves, born in May and June, usually stay with the mother through the following winter.

OTHER MAMMALS TO LOOK FOR

Fisher
- about dog-size, 1 m total length, tail 1/3 total length
- dark brown, slender, bushy tail, short legs
- not common, increasing in numbers, reported in every county of mainland Nova Scotia
- evergreen forests, near water, travelling into deciduous woods of new growth

Marten
-about size of domestic cat, 60 to 65 cm total length, tail 1/3 total length
-yellowish-brown, darker on tail and legs, prominent orange throat patch
-long, slender body, short legs, bushy tail
-rare, more common in eastern and southern counties and in Cape Breton
-once fairly common, has now been reintroduced
-deep, coniferous woods, not in areas of new growth

Cougar or Mountain Lion
-large, long-tailed cat; head-body length 1.2 to 1.8 m, tail 60 to 90 cm; resembling a female African lion; the only wild cat with a tail that is more than 1/3 its total length
-remote and rocky forests, deer habitats
-sightings by reliable observers are reported from time to time

CHECK LIST OF WINTER MAMMALS

The following list includes those mammals that are active in Nova Scotia during the winter. Some species are common throughout the province, others are very rare or are present in certain localities only. The list does not include sea mammals, bats (which are either hibernating or have migrated south), or other hibernating mammals such as bears, jumping mice, and chipmunks.

Species	Date First Observed	Location First Observed
Masked Shrew		
Smoky Shrew		
American Water Shrew		
Arctic Shrew		
Pigmy Shrew		
Short-tailed Shrew		
Star-nosed Mole		
Snowshoe Hare (Rabbit)		
Woodchuck		
Red Squirrel		
Northern Flying Squirrel		
Beaver		
Deer Mouse		
White-footed Mouse		
Red-backed Vole		
Muskrat		
Meadow Vole		
Brown Rat		
House Mouse		
Porcupine		
Red Fox		
Raccoon		
Marten		
Fisher		
Short-tailed Weasel (Ermine)		

Species	Date First Observed	Location First Observed
Mink		
Striped Skunk		
Otter		
Cougar		
Lynx		
Bobcat		
White-tailed Deer		
Moose		

GUIDE TO MAMMALS TRACKS

Animal tracks are frequently encountered in our woodlands and fields. It is sometimes difficult to identify the tracks and often the identification is based on educated guesses. If you find a good trail, try to follow it. It is fun and a challenge to learn where the animal lives and what it was doing.

You will not likely find complete prints except in damp, firm mud. Winter weather conditions add many complications. If the temperature is above or near freezing, a small track will melt around the edges and appear to be a much larger track. For example, the track of a domestic cat may melt to a size approaching that of a bobcat. Lightly drifting snow may cover the claw marks of a dog's track so that it resembles the print of a cat.

For descriptive purposes, the tracks are divided into 6 groups. Each group is then subdivided primarily by size of the print and width of the straddle. The term straddle refers to the width of the track; that is, to the distance from the outside of the right footprint to the outside of the left footprint. Straddle measurements for a species are fairly constant, although some variation is seen based on gait and size of the individual. Stride, the distance from one set of prints to the next, is not used in these descriptions because it varies greatly with the speed and gait of the animal. However, stride should be examined, as it will help determine the size of the animal in question. Habitat and size are the easiest ways of reducing the number of choices when making an identification.

GROUP 1:   Hoofed, one rounded print, "V" mark
            at back of print, may be shod .... page 104

GROUP 2:   Hoofed, 2 pointed toes .... page 105

GROUP 3:   Tracks roughly circular, more or less
            in a straight line, 4 toes in print .... page 106

GROUP 4:   Tracks in pairs, usually widely spaced,
            5 toes in print .... page 107

GROUP 5:   Tracks in groups of 4, 2 large and 2
            small; in distinct tracks, front foot
            shows 4 toes and hind foot shows 5 toes .. page 108

GROUP 6:   Sole of foot large and distinct, toes
            appear separate, hind feet large and
            usually overlap prints made by smaller
            front feet .... page 110

GROUP 1: Hoofed, one rounded print, "V" mark at back of print, may be shod .... Pony or Horse

GROUP 1

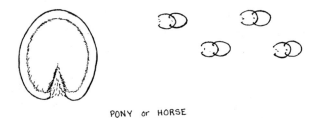

PONY or HORSE

GROUP 2:   Hoofed, 2 pointed toes
- print about 5 to 6 cm long, short
steps, near civilization .... Domestic Goat
- print about 7 to 8 cm long, short
steps, near civilization .... Domestic Sheep
- print about 7 to 9 cm long, long
steps, more remote .... White-tailed Deer, page 97
- print 10 to 13 cm long, rounded,
near civilization .... Domestic Cow
- print 13 to 16 cm long, pointed,
remote .... Moose, page 99

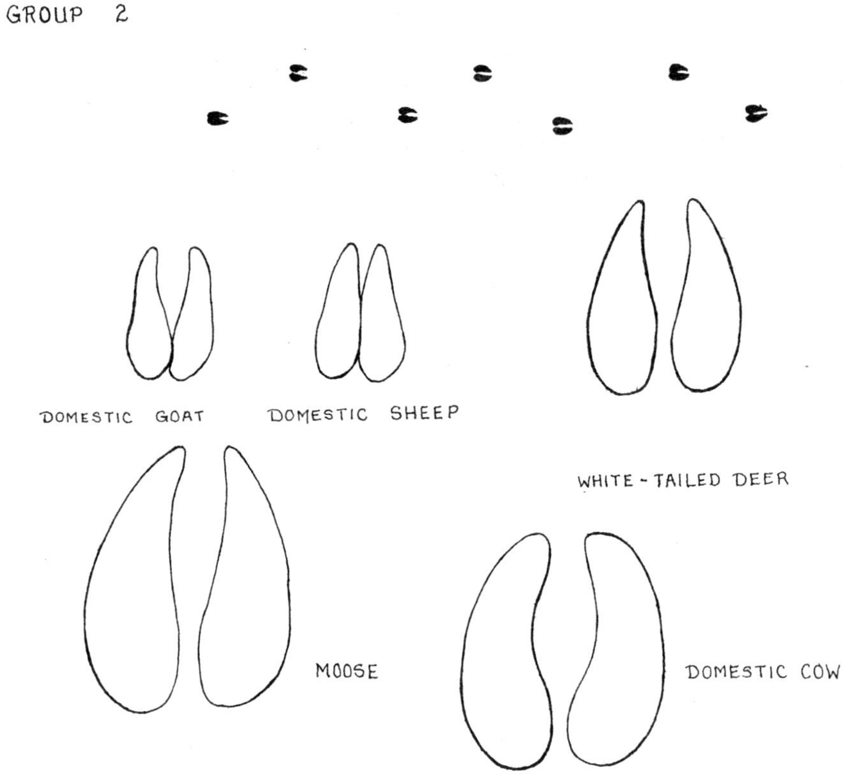

GROUP 2

DOMESTIC GOAT   DOMESTIC SHEEP

WHITE-TAILED DEER

MOOSE   DOMESTIC COW

105

GROUP 3: Tracks roughly circular, more or less in a straight line, 4 toes in print

　　a) no claw marks showing (cat family)

- print about 3 cm long, straddle
  about 7 cm .... Domestic Cat
- print 5 to 6 cm long, straddle
  about 12 cm .... Bobcat, page 95
- print 8 to 10 cm long, straddle
  about 18 cm .... Lynx, page 94

　　b) claw marks showing, print more oval (dog family)

- size variable, drag marks of
  feet may show, route running
  back and forth .... Domestic Dog
- print 5 to 6 cm long; straddle
  8 to 12 cm; no drag marks; route
  direct and along borders, fences,
  etc.; clear tracks show curved
  ridge on heel pad .... Red Fox, page 88

GROUP 3

DOMESTIC CAT　　　　BOBCAT　　　　LYNX

DOMESTIC DOG　　　RED FOX

106

GROUP 4: Tracks in pairs, usually widely spaced, 5 toes in print (Weasels)

GROUP 4

WEASELS

SKUNK

MINK

OTTER

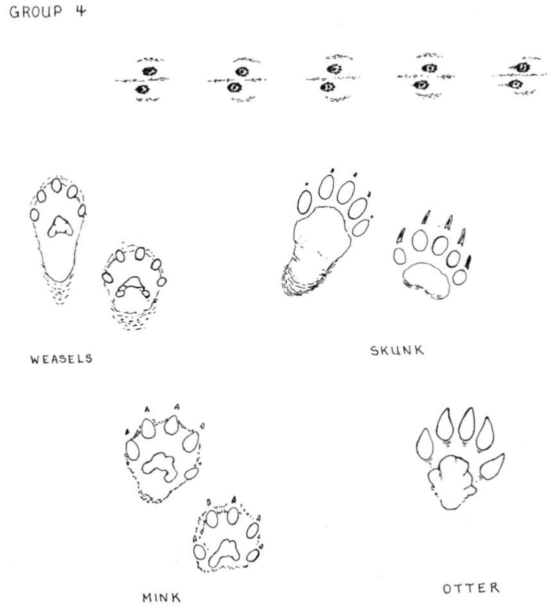

GROUP 5:   Tracks in groups of 4, 2 large and 2 small; in
            distinct tracks, front foot shows 4 toes and
            hind foot shows 5 toes (Rodents)

- larger track about 1 cm long,
  straddle about 2 cm .... Mice, Moles,
                                    Shrews (see notes below)
- larger track 4 to 5 cm long,
  straddle 6 to 8 cm, front foot
  prints side-by side .... Squirrels (see notes below)
- larger track about 3 cm long,
  straddle 6 to 7 cm, tail drags,
  toes and sole showing, builds
  tunnels and runways, near
  civilization .... Brown Rat, page 85
- larger track about 5 cm long,
  straddle 8 to 12 cm, in fields
  and along woodland borders .... Woodchuck, page 77
- larger track 10 to 15 cm long,
  front foot prints one in front
  of other, straddle 12 to 18 cm .... Hare, page 76

Notes — The tracks of mice, moles and shrews are difficult to identify
with certainty and no attempt is made here to describe the differences
in detail. The habitat, however, is helpful. The Deer Mouse is
generally more common in deciduous habitats and around woodland
cabins (page 81), and the Red-backed Vole is more common in
evergreen woods, although there is overlap between the two species.
Tracks of the Deer Mouse usually show the drag marks of its long
tail. The tail of the Red-backed Vole is shorter and drag marks do not
usually show. The Meadow Vole (page 84) is found in fields, and
burrows beneath the snow where it constructs grassy nests on the
surface of the ground. The House Mouse (page 86) is found only near
human dwellings. Moles and Shrews tunnel underground or under
the snow and infrequently come to the surface. Their tracks are
uncommon and are usually associated with tunnels.

   Squirrel tracks "appear" and "disappear" as the animal runs
from tree to tree. Squirrels dig through the snow in search of seeds
and nuts. They also feed on cones, and piles of cone scales often help
confirm the identification of squirrel tracks. Flying Squirrel (page 79)
tracks are the same as those of the Red Squirrel (page 78) except that
a "landing mark" can usually be found.

GROUP 5

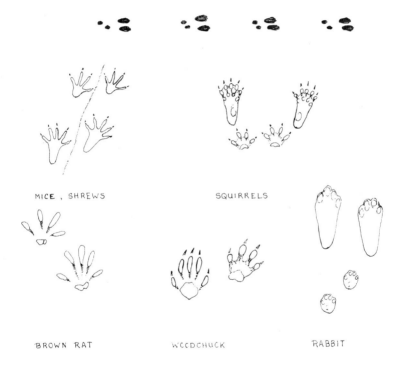

MICE , SHREWS   SQUIRRELS

BROWN RAT   WOODCHUCK   RABBIT

109

GROUP 6: Sole of foot large and distinct, toes appear separate, hind feet large and usually overlap prints made by smaller front feet

- hind track 4 to 8 cm long, straddle 8 to 10 cm, usually 4 toes only showing on front foot, sole elongate, tail drags, near water .... Muskrat, page 83

- hind track 8 to 10 cm long, straddle 9 to 13 cm, sole rounded, toes long, large print of hind foot usually beside small print of front foot .... Raccoon, page 89

- hind track 12 to 17 cm long, straddle 15 to 20 cm, hind foot wide with webbed toes and narrow heel for padding, plows trough in snow, broad tail drags obliterating tracks, near water, usually in poplar stand with cut trees and peeled branches, beaver lodge and dam nearby. (Beavers store food in the water before freezing and it is not necessary for them to make frequent trips along the shore in the winter. Thus, their tracks are not always evident although the animals may be present in the area.) .... Beaver, page 80

- sole of hind track 6 to 8 cm long, straddle 20 to 25 cm, sole twice as long as wide, toes not conspicuous, prints alternate and swing inward, tail drags and swings leaving quill marks in the snow, route ends at tree .... Porcupine, page 87

GROUP 6

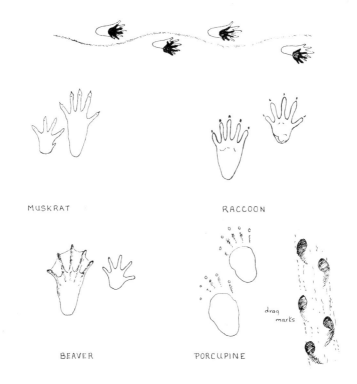

MUSKRAT

RACCOON

BEAVER

PORCUPINE

drag marks

TREES and SHRUBS

For description, a tree is a woody plant that usually has a single main trunk and that is usually more than 5 or 6 metres in height. A shrub is a woody plant that is divided into several main branches near the ground and that is less than 5 or 6 metres in height. These definitions are intended to provide a general organization for these *Notes,* but they lack preciseness when applied to individual species and specimens. For example, some "shrubs" become large and tree-like in form, some young trees may be clustered and appear to have several trunks, and young growth from tree stumps may show shrub-like features. Height is also used as a means of grouping trees and shrubs for identification. Again, young trees and shrubs may not have attained their full height and specimens growing under adverse conditions may be stunted. Thus, until the characteristics of the major groups of woody plants are familiar, it may be necessary to try one or two of the tree or shrub groups described below when identifying an unknown specimen. Again, remember that there are a number of trees and shrubs in Nova Scotia that are not included in these *Nature Notes* . Since these may "key out" incorrectly with the guides given below, the full descriptions and illustrations should always be checked.

The descriptions of the trees and shrubs in *Nature Notes* are primarily based on features of the twigs, buds and leaf scars. These features are usually readily visible, but the use of a hand lens will often assist in making the identification. Although an attempt is made to limit the use of scientific terms, an understanding of several is helpful. With reference to the illustration, these are:

Twig - The terminal portion of the branch. Comparing different species, the twig may vary in color, it may be smooth or hairy, straight or zig-zag, and stout or slender. In some species the taste and odor of crushed twigs is distinctive.

Nodes - the areas along the twig at which the leaves and buds are attached.

Buds - the buds are the undeveloped shoots that remain in a dormant state over winter. The bud is covered by bud scales which are reduced leaves modified to protect the underlying tissues. The terminal bud is at the tip of the branch, and the lateral buds are distributed along the sides of the branch. Comparing species, buds vary in color and size, they may be pointed or rounded, smooth or hairy, and shiny or sticky. Deciduous trees and shrubs are divided into two main groups: those in which the lateral buds are arranged opposite to one another, and those in which the positions of the lateral buds alternate along the stem.

112

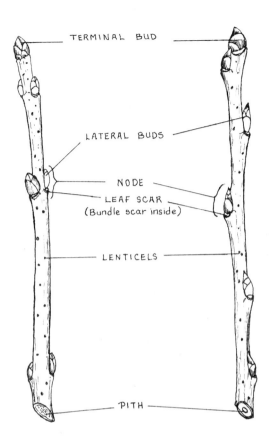

TERMINAL BUD

LATERAL BUDS

NODE

LEAF SCAR
(Bundle scar inside)

LENTICELS

PITH

BUDS OPPOSITE   BUDS ALTERNATE

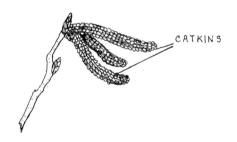

CATKINS

113

Leaf Scar - the site of attachment of the leaf. Most Nova Scotian trees and shrubs are deciduous, losing their leaves each autumn. Before the leaf falls a corky layer is formed to seal off the underlying tissues. This becomes the leaf scar. Comparing species, leaf scars may be small or conspicuous and they may be oval, elongate, crescent-shaped, U-shaped, or horse-shoe shaped.

Bundle Scars - bundle scars appear as small marks inside the leaf scar. Bundle scars are the sealed ends of the bundles of tubules that passed from the twig to the leaf. Comparing species, the leaf scar may contain one or several bundle scars, and the bundle scars may be rounded, crescent or elongate in shape.

Pith - the pith forms the central core of the twig. It is used in these *Notes* only if its shape or color provide clues which aid in identification.

Lenticels - small pores distributed over the surface of the twig that admit air to the underlying tissues. In many species they are not conspicuous. In others they are a useful aid to identification. Comparing species, they may be round or elongate, various colors, and they may be smooth or form rough, wart-like elevations.

Catkin - a cluster of small flowers or fruit. May be upright or hanging. The sexes are usually separate. The male or staminate (pollen) catkins for the coming season are often at the end of the twig. The female or pistillate catkins form along the twig and usually do not become conspicuous until spring. Dried female cones from the previous season may be present and the cones of some species open and release seeds during the winter.

NOTES

TREES

About 30 species of trees are native to Nova Scotia and others have been introduced for ornamental or agricultural purposes. *Nature Notes* includes those native species that are commonly found in the woodlands. Only a few of the introduced species are included, those frequently seen about the countryside.

GUIDE TO THE TREES

For identification purposes, the trees are divided into 5 main groups. Each group is then subdivided by listing several characteristics that help identify the tree.

GROUP 1:   Conifers, needle-like green leaves
usually present, cones often present;
or cones usually present if needles
absent .... see "Guide to the Conifers", page 123

GROUP 2:   Deciduous, leaf scars and buds
oppositely arranged .... page 116

GROUP 3:   Deciduous, leaf scars and buds
alternately arranged, buds 1 cm
or more in length .... page 117

GROUP 4:   Deciduous, leaf scars and buds
alternately arranged, buds less
than 1 cm long, end bud placed
in centre of twig tip .... page 117

GROUP 5:   Deciduous, leaf scars and buds
alternately arranged, buds less
than 1 cm long, end bud absent
or placed to one side of twig tip .... page 118

GROUP 2:   **Deciduous trees, leaf scars and buds oppositely arranged**

a.   Terminal bud large (more
than 1 cm), chestnut coloured,
sticky; leaf scars large and
horse-shoe shaped .... Horse Chestnut, page 181

b.   Terminal bud small (less than
1 cm), dark brown almost black,
rounded; leaf scars prominent .... Ashes, page 192

c.   Terminal bud small (about 1 cm
or less), brown or reddish,
elliptical; leaf scars small .... Maples, page 178

GROUP 3:   **Deciduous trees, leaf scars and buds alternately
arranged, buds 1 cm or more long**

a.   Terminal bud thick, gummy,
fragrant when crushed; pith
star-shaped .... Balsam Poplar, page 140

b.   Buds 1 to 2 cm or more long,
slender and sharp, pointing
away from twig .... Beech, page 155

c.   Buds 1 to 2 cm long, slender
and sharp, pressed against
twig .... Shadbush, page 165

d.   Buds not covered by scales,
hairy; two terminal buds,
one stalked and twice as long
as other .... Witch-Hazel, page 159

GROUP 4:   **Deciduous trees, leaf scars and buds alternately
arranged, buds less than 1 cm long, end bud placed in
centre of twig tip**

a.   Trees and shrubs with long,
sharp thorns .... Hawthorn, page 166

b.   Young twigs orange, small woody
knobs along twigs, small rounded
buds often clustered on spur
branches, small cones usually
present .... Larch, page 131

c.   Twigs zig-zagging from bud to
bud; older bark white or
yellowish, sometimes peeling
into papery thin strips,
horizontal lenticles
conspicuous, catkins present
at end of twigs .... Birch, page 149

d.   Twigs zig-zagging from bud to bud;
bark grey-brown , scaly and curled,
lenticels not conspicuous, catkins
present at end of twigs .... Ironwood, page 148

e. Twigs straight, twigs five-angled
(roll between fingers), young bark
yellowish-green, pith star-shaped
in cross-section . . . . Poplar, page 139

f. Twigs straight, terminal and
lateral buds clustered at twig
end; large, lobed, withered leaves
often present, acorns sometimes
present . . . . Oak, page 156

g. Twigs straight; bark smooth, dark,
showing reddish tinge or orange
underbark, horizontal lenticels
conspicuous; trees or shrubs;
black knot fungus often present . . . . Cherries, page 170

h. Twigs straight; buds rounded,
clustered on small spur-like
branches; buds and twig tip hairy . . . . Apple, page 162

i. Twigs straight; twigs reddish-
brown with white lenticels;
older bark grey; terminal bud
large, oblong, hairy, sticky . . . . Mountain Ash, page 164

**GROUP 5: Deciduous trees, leaf scars and buds alternately
arranged, buds less than 1 cm long, end bud absent or
placed to one side of twig tip**

a. buds covered with a single cap-
like scale . . . . Willow, page 138

b. buds covered with several scales;
larger end buds rounded, green or
red; bud shape asymmetrical . . . . Basswood, page 182

c. buds covered with several scales,
buds reddish-brown and pointed,
bud shape symmetrical . . . . Elm, page 157

d. buds covered with leaf scar,
spines or thorns usually present,
trees or shrubs . . . . Locusts, page 173

118

SHRUBS

More than 40 genera of non-cultivated shrubs and small woody plants occur in Nova Scotia and most of these include several species and varieties. Of these, 25 genera are represented, sometimes by more than one species, in *Nature Notes*. These were selected because they are commonly found or, if less common, because their colours or berries attract special attention. Shrubs imported for ornamental purposes are not included unless they are common escapees and are frequently found in the wild state.

GUIDE TO THE SHRUBS

For identification purposes, the shrubs are divided into 7 main groups. Each group is then subdivided by listing several characteristics that help identify each shrub.

GROUP 1:   **Evergreen shrubs, either needle-like or broad green leaves present**

a.   Twigs flattened with needles along sides, needles with green

stems partially encircling twig,
green buds on undersurface .... Yew, page 125

b. Needles grouped in 3's,
blue berry .... Juniper, page 137

c. Broad leaves clustered toward
end of twig, leaves opposite
or whorled in 3's .... Laurels, page 187

d. Broad leaves, leathery above,
dense wooly brown below, margins
rolled under .... Labrador Tea, page 185

e. Broad leaves, 1 to 3 cm long, low
trailing shrub .... Bearberry, page 188

f. Broad leaves, 1 cm long, low
trailing shrub .... Cranberry, page 190

GROUP 2: **Deciduous shrubs, leaf scars and buds opposite or whorled**

a. leaf scars clustered toward
end of twig, broad green leaves
usually present (evergreen) .... Laurel, page 187

b. Bark bright red .... Red Osier, page 184

c. Twigs stout and angled, pith
large and white or brown,
lenticels conspicuous, single
terminal bud usually replaced
by a pair of buds, ends of
twigs often dead .... Elderberries, page 196

d. Twigs smooth and slender, pith
small, lenticels white and small,
single terminal bud usually-
replaced by a pair of greenish
or reddish buds .... Lilac, page 193

e. Buds oval, elongate and sometimes twisting around stem,
stalked, often undeveloped
green leaves visible .... Viburnums, page 195

GROUP 3: **Deciduous shrubs, buds covered by leaf scar, short thorns on either side of leaf scar, leaf scars alternating** Clammy Locust, page 173

120

GROUP 4: **Deciduous shrubs, leaf scars and buds alternating, thorns or prickles present**

a. Thorns 2 cm or more in length .... Hawthorns, page 166

b. Thorns single or branched into 3's, underbark bright yellow .... Barberry, page 158

c. In thickets, canes lined with either stiff bristles or prickles or both, no leaf scars, stems of leaves often persisting, remains of influorescences present .... Raspberry and Blackberry, page 167

d. Twigs with stiff prickles or short decurved thorns, leaf scars narrow, fleshy red fruit often persisting .... Rose, page 168

GROUP 5: **Deciduous shrubs, leaf scars and buds alternating, no thorns or prickles, 1 m or less in height**

a. Large terminal bud, yellow or pink; small lateral buds clustered at end of season's growth, old fruit capsules persisting .... Rhodora, page 186

b. Twigs slender, greenish or reddish, with raised granules; top twigs much branched, leaves sometimes persist, buds small .... Blueberry, page 190

c. Twigs slender and wand-like, twig ends frequently winter-killed, clusters of dried flowers or fruit often persisting at twig ends, buds small .... Spirea, page 161

d. Young twigs yellowish dotted with resin droplets, upcurved, withered fern-like leaves often present, fruit persisting as a burr, hairy catkins at twig ends .... Sweetfern, page 146

e. Young twigs dotted with resin droplets, bluish berries

121

covered with white wax, twigs
clustered at ends of stems,
withered leaves may persist .... Bayberries, page 144

GROUP 6: **Deciduous shrubs, leaf scars and buds alternating, no
thorns or prickles, more than one metre in height, buds
more than 0.5 cm long**

a. Buds without scales; 2 buds
at twig ends, one stalked
and twice as long as other,
fruit capsules present .... Witch-Hazel, page 159

b. Buds covered with a single
scale .... Willows, page 138

c. Buds covered with many scales;
buds long, pointed, pressed
against twig .... Shadbush, page 165

d. Buds covered with many scales,
catkins and woody cones present;
triangular pith .... Alders, page 154

e. Buds densely hairy, grey; twigs
reddish-brown; catkins present;
fruit enclosed in a tubular husk
may be present .... Hazelnut, page 147

f. Shrubs flat topped; young branches
velvety hairy, brownish; fruit
densely hairy, red spike at end
of branch .... Sumac, page 174

GROUP 7: **Deciduous shrubs, leaf scars and buds alternating, no
thorns or prickles, more than 1 metre in height, buds
0.5 cm or less long**

a. Young twigs dotted with resin
droplets, bluish berries covered
with white wax, twigs clustered
at ends of stems, withered leaves
may persist .... Bayberries, page 144

b. Smooth bark showing reddish
tinge, horizontal white or orange
lenticels, often infested with
black knot, twigs and bark with
bitter almond taste and odor .... Cherries, page 170

122

c.   Twigs greenish often streaked
    with white, leaf scars crowded   Alternate-leaved
    at twig ends .... Dogwood, page 184

d.   Ash coloured bark, sometimes
    mottled; buds clustered at
    twig ends, twigs angular,
    stubby spur twigs, red berries
    may be present .... Canada Holly, page 175

e.   Ash-grey bark, young twigs
    purplish with whitish bloom,
    buds and leaf scars clustered
    at twig ends or on spur twigs,
    fruit red persisting into
    winter .... Mountain Holly, page 176

f.   Buds dark red, pointed,
    against twig .... Chokeberry, page 163

**Group 1: Conifers, needle-like green leaves usually present, cones
often present; or cones usually present if needles absent**

Conifers

The coniferous trees, or softwoods, include the Pines, Spruces, Larch, Hemlock, Fir and Cedar. Two shrubs, Yew and Juniper, are also conifers.

The leaves of the conifers are in the form of needles or scales. The needles remain on the tree for 2 or 3 years. Because the needles do not all fall from the tree at the same time, as do the leaves of deciduous trees, the conifers are also called *evergreen trees.* The one exception is the Larch or Tamarack which loses all of its needles each autumn.

Conifers are tall, straight, spire-like trees. The branches are usually arranged in whorls around the trunk. While it is not an exact means of aging a conifer, the number of whorls of branches along the trunk will give a general indication of the age of the tree.

The conifers are so called because they bear cones. The cones are the fruit, and winged seeds develop at the base of the scales. The cones begin to form in spring and, for most conifers, the seeds are released in autumn. The cones of Pines, on the other hand, require two years to develop and the seeds may be released during the second season or, depending upon the species, the cones may remain closed retaining the seeds for several years. Yew and Juniper do not bear the usual cone-type fruit. Yew has a fleshy red berry and Juniper has a waxy blue berry. While these fruit look like berries, they are, in strict

123

botanical terms, cones which have been modified by the thickening and fusion of the scales.

Guide to the Conifers

124

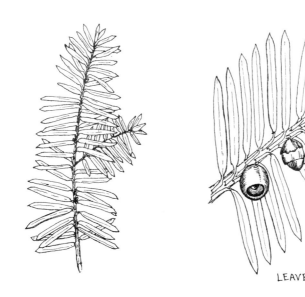

LEAVES and FRUIT

CANADA YEW
(Taxus canadensis)

Description
- 1 to 1.5 m in height, often forming low ground cover
- needles flattened, 1 to 2.5 cm long, needles with stems which partially encircle twigs, dark green, pointed and arranged along sides of twig so that the twig appears flattened
- fruit a red waxy berry, usually shed in autumn
- winter buds greenish, on undersurface of twig

Habitat
- throughout Nova Scotia, shady, damp woodlands
- under other conifers, rocky sites

Notes
- Canada Yew resembles hemlock and is also called ground hemlock. The fruit which looks like a fleshy berry is actually a modified cone and the Yew is a conifer. Yew is a favourite browse for deer and moose.

125

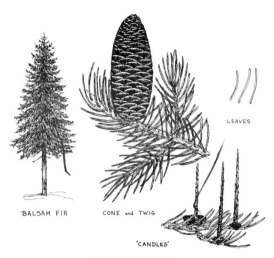

BALSAM FIR

CONE and TWIG

LEAVES

'CANDLES'

BALSAM FIR
(Abies balsamea)

Description
- small to medium-sized tree, branches arranged in whorls
- needles flat, 2 to 2.5 cm long, blunt (spruce needles are pointed), 2 white lines along undersurface, arranged along sides of twig giving twig a flat appearance, needles without stems (hemlock needles have stems)
- twigs smooth with no woody needle pegs (twigs rough with woody pegs in spruce and hemlock)
- cones cylindrical, 5 to 10 cm long, upright not hanging as in spruce and hemlock, cone scales fall in autumn leaving central cone stem standing on twig (candles) unlike other conifers in which the entire cone falls
- young bark smooth, greenish with silvery areas, resin blisters present; old bark dark brown with reddish tinge, furrowed, small scales

Habitat
- common throughout Nova Scotia, damp, open sites
- pure or mixed stands, reforests cut areas and abandoned fields

Notes
- Balsam Fir is valuable for pulpwood. Fir may live for more than 100 years but is usually replaced by spruces and hardwoods as part of natural tree succession when it is about 30 cm in diameter. Fir is the preferred Christmas tree because of its symmetry, fragrance, and because it holds its needles longer than do spruces if the trunk is freshly cut and placed in water with a little sugar added. Fir seeds are eaten by birds, and several mammals browse on the twigs or eat the bark. Patches stripped of bark by porcupines are frequently seen.

126

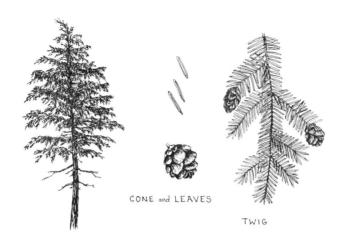

CONE and LEAVES

TWIG

EASTERN HEMLOCK
(Tsuga canadensis)

Description
- large tree, drooping branches not arranged in whorls as other conifers, top not erect but falling to one side
- needles flattened, attached along sides of twig so that twig appears flat, 2 cm or less long, blunt, 2 white lines along undersurface, each needle has a short stem attaching it to woody peg on twig
- twigs yellowish-brown, hairy, needle scars raised woody pegs
- cones small, 2 cm or less long, hanging at ends of twigs, seeds shed in autumn, cones fall in late winter and early spring
- bark brown, furrowed in old trees, inner bark reddish

Habitat
- throughout Nova Scotia, more common in southwestern counties and Annapolis Valley
- sandy, moist habitats; often in ravines and along river banks

Notes
- Hemlock is cut for pulpwood and for rough lumber. Hemlock once grew in pure stands in which the trees reached a diameter of more than 1 m. Such large trees can still be found. Hemlock is frequently planted as an ornamental and can be trimmed when used in hedges. Hemlock tea, prepared by adding the needles to boiling water and steeping to taste preference, is an aromatic and tasty treat while winter camping and cooking over an open fire. The seeds are eaten by squirrels, mice and a number of birds, and the twigs are browsed by deer and rabbits. Ruffed Grouse frequently use the shelter afforded by hemlock stands during the winter.

127

WHITE SPRUCE   CONE - LEAVES   TWIG

SPRUCES

The White, Red, and Black Spruces are native to Nova Scotia, and are widespread throughout the province. Several other spruces are planted as ornamentals but are not found in the woodlands, and are not included in *Nature Notes.*

WHITE SPRUCE
(Picea glauca)

Description
- medium to tall tree, pyramidal in shape, higher branches curving upward, lower branches drooping often to ground
- needles bluish-green, pointed, 2 cm or less long, on woody pegs giving stem a rough surface, crowded on upper surface of twig
- cones cylindrical, 5 to 8 cm long (longer than other spruces), hanging, cone scales have a smooth edge
- seeds released in early winter, cones remain one year and fall in early winter
- twigs smooth, not hairy
- bark brown-grey, sometimes with silvery bloom; scaly, resin around wounds

Habitat
- common throughout Nova Scotia, gravelly and sandy habitats

Notes
- White Spruce grows rapidly and often invades abandoned fields. It is, consequently, also called pasture spruce. It is used for pulp and lumber. Spruce dries and loses its needles too quickly to be of value as a Christmas tree. Its seeds are eaten by squirrels and many species of birds. Birds and mammals seek the shelter of spruce trees during the winter. The thick foliage provides protection from the wind, and the drooping boughs hold the snow, "roofing" sheltered pockets underneath. Deer, rabbits, grouse and pheasants are often found in these spruce shelters.

128

CONE   LEAVES   TWIG

RED SPRUCE

RED SPRUCE
(Picea rubens)

Description
- small to medium-sized tree, branches open with upcurved ends
- needles yellowish-green, pointed, 2 cm or less long, mounted on woody pegs giving stem a rough surface, mostly on sides and upper surfaces of twig
- cones oval shaped, 2 to 4 cm long, hanging at top of tree, fall during late autumn and early winter and not present during late winter, cone scales wavy
- twigs yellowish, hairy
- bark dark brown, reddish tinge, scaly

Habitat
- throughout Nova Scotia, more common in central part of province
- open, drained habitats; reduced growth in shady, wet sites

Notes
- The Red Spruce is used for pulpwood and lumber. Young twigs and needles are used to make spruce beer and the hardened resin is good spruce gum. It can be distinguished from white spruce by its hairy twigs and by its small, ovoid cones. It can be distinguished from the black spruce by its yellowish green foliage, longer needles, and by the fact that it usually loses its cones each autumn whereas the black spruce retains open cones for several years. Habitat assists in the identification, Red Spruce is more common in the dryer uplands and the black spruce in wet lowlands.

129

CONE   LEAVES   TWIG

BLACK SPRUCE
(Picea mariana)

Description
- small to medium-sized tree, slender, short branches
- needles shorter than other spruces, 6 to 8 mm long, mounted on woody pegs, curving upward
- cones hanging from ends of branches, 1.5 to 4 cm long, oval to almost round when open, cone scales rough edged, remain on trees for several years
- twigs brown, hairy
- bark dark brown, reddish tinge, scaly and flaking

Habitat
- common throughout Nova Scotia, stunted in extremely rocky or wet habitats
- lowlands, wet soils, swamps, bogs, along coast

Notes
- The wood of Black Spruce warps easily and is used only for pulp and rough construction. The wood can be bent and is used for making bows for frames, lobster pots, etc. The hardened resin of Black Spruce makes good spruce gum, and the young twigs and needles are used to make spruce beer. Black Spruce is difficult to distinguish from red spruce (see red spruce).

130

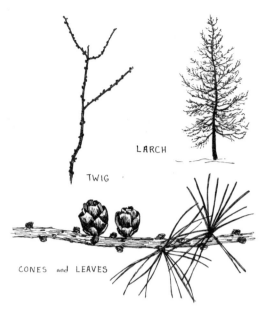

LARCH

TWIG

CONES and LEAVES

LARCH
(Larix laricina)

Description
- small to medium-sized tree with open, drooping branches
- needles fall in autumn, absent in winter; weathered and dried needles may be present, in bundles of 2, 2 to 3 cm long, near twig end or clustered on spur twigs and knobs
- cones upright, rounded, less than 3 cm long, seeds shed in autumn and open cones present in winter
- twigs orange-brown, lined with needle scars, spur twigs and knobs present
- buds small, clustered on spur branches, and twig ends
- bark dark brown, reddish tinge, scaly

Habitat
- common throughout Nova Scotia
- open sites, dry and wet soils, swamps and bogs, abandoned fields

Notes
- Larch is also called tamarack and hackmatack. It is the only conifer in Nova Scotia that sheds its needles in autumn; the needles turn yellow and fall usually in November. Its wood is hard and has an oily texture which protects it against moisture. This natural preservative makes Larch a preferred wood for fence posts, poles, etc. The seeds, buds and twigs are eaten by a number of birds and mammals, and porcupines frequently strip the bark.

131

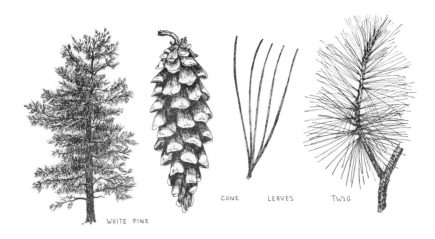

CONE   LEAVES   TWIG

WHITE PINE

PINES

Four types of pines are present in Nova Scotia. The White, Red and Jack Pines are native to the province. The Scotch Pine is an introduced species.

WHITE PINE
(Pinus strobus)

Description
- tall, straight tree
- needles in bundles of 5, 4 to 8 cm long
- cones elongate, 10 to 20 cm long, hanging, seeds released in autumn of second season
- young bark smooth, greenish; old bark dark brown, furrowed

Habitat
- throughout Nova Scotia, preferring sand and gravelly habitats

Notes
- The White Pine is our most abundant pine. It may grow to over 30 m in height and was once in demand by ship builders for masts. It is a valuable timber tree, its wood being used for general construction, interior finishing, and furniture. The terminal shoots of this species may be deformed by attacks of an insect, the white pine weevil. The White Pine is an important food source for wildlife. Many birds, such as chickadees and grosbeaks, eat the seeds. Squirrels and mice eat the seeds and buds and several large mammals, such as porcupine and deer, browse on the bark, twigs and needles.

132

TWIG   LEAVES   CONE   RED PINE

RED PINE
(Pinus resinosa)

Description
- tall, straight tree, lower branches usually dead
- needles in bundles of 2, 7 to 15 cm long
- cones oval, almost round, 10 cm or less long; seeds released in spring of second year
- bark reddish or yellowish-brown; old bark furrowed, scaly, underbark reddish

Habitat
- throughout Nova Scotia, preferring dry sand and gravel habitats

Notes
- The Red Pine is a valuable timber tree. Its grain has a reddish tinge and it is used less for interior finishing and furniture than is white pine. The wood is porous and easily preserved (creosoted) and is used for poles, ties, cribbings, etc. Red Pine may grow to over 30 m in height and, like white pine, was once in demand by ship builders for masts. Red Pine grows rapidly and is commonly used in reforestation projects. Like white pine, the Red Pine is an important winter food source for many birds and mammals.

133

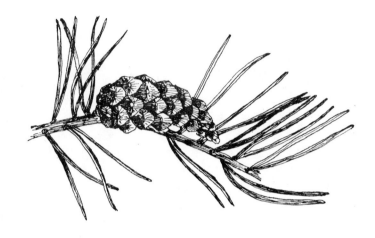

JACK PINE
(Pinus banksiana)

Description
- medium-sized tree, stunted in poor habitats
- needles in bundles of 2, 2 to 4 cm long, twisted, flattened
- cones 4 to 5 cm long, cone scales pointed, many cones curving into stem and pointing towards end of branch
  young bark dark brown, reddish; old bark greyish-brown, furrowed

Habitat
- scattered through Nova Scotia, locally common, more common in central counties and near the New Brunswick border
- in wet, sandy or rocky soils

Notes
- Jack Pine is not plentiful enough to be of economic importance. It may reforest after fire or heavy cutting. The cones may remain closed for several years, but will open, perhaps stimulated by the heat from a light ground fire, and release all the seeds at the same time. For this reason, Jack Pine often occurs in stands of even-aged trees.

134

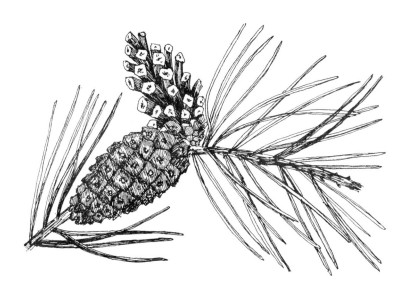

SCOTCH PINE
(Pinus sylvestris)

Description
- small tree, highly branched and twisted
- needles in bundles of 2, 3 to 7 cm long, pointed, twisted upper surface rounded
- cones elongate, scales pyramid-shaped, many cones pointing downward or towards trunk
- young bark yellowish-brown; old bark greyish-brown, rough

Habitat
- planted throughout Nova Scotia, prefers sand or gravel

Notes
- Scotch Pine is not native to Novs Scotia but is planted for ornamental purposes and Christmas trees. It is sometimes planted in areas of erosion for it grows quickly and its lower branches spread to form a ground cover. Scotch Pine is too uncommon and is too twisted to be of value as a lumber tree. The lower branches provide shelter for wildlife and several species, especially pheasants, will be seen in thickets of Scotch Pine.

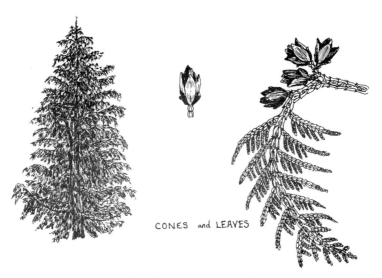

CONES and LEAVES

NORTHERN WHITE CEDAR
(Thuja occidentalis)

Description

- small tree, lower branches spreading, upper branches often upcurved giving the tree a pyramid shape
- needles scale-like, 0.3 cm long, fragrant, covering twig and not standing out as in other conifers
- cones upright, 1 to 2 cm long, seeds shed in early autumn and open cones on trees during winter
- young bark reddish-brown; old bark shredding, inner layers fibrous

Habitat

- rare, scattered throughout Nova Scotia, more common in western counties, Annapolis Valley, and near New Brunswick border
- frequently planted about homes
- in wild, prefers sunny, wet, and rocky habitats

Notes

- Naturally occurring White Cedar is not plentiful in Nova Scotia, although it is common in New Brunswick. It is planted for ornamental purposes and hedges. The wood is resistent to decay and is used for posts and, since it splits cleanly, for shingles. Cedar wood is reddish-brown and fragrant and is of value for interior trim, making chests, etc. The wood is light-weight but strong and is used for building canoes and small boats.

136

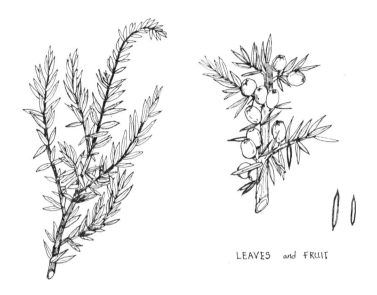

LEAVES and FRUIT

JUNIPER
(Juniperus communis)

Description
- low, creeping shrub, branches upcurved
- needles 1 to 2 cm long, rigid and pointed, in 3's, flattened, upper surface grooved with white line
- fruit a blue berry, often covered with a whitish film which will rub off
- older branches brown, bark scaly

Habitat
- throughout Nova Scotia, dry and sunny areas
- abandoned fields and pastures, open and rocky woods, along roadsides

Notes
- The Juniper is a spreading shrub which may form a thick ground cover over much of the field. It is a conifer because the blue berry is, in botanical terms, a modified cone. It may be planted as a decorative shrub. The berries and buds are eaten by birds such as pheasants, and the twigs are browsed by deer, moose and other mammals.

137

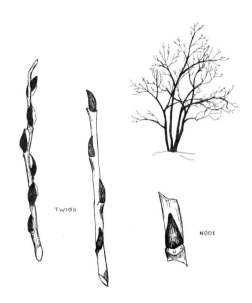

TWIGS

NODE

WILLOW FAMILY

The willow family includes the well-known willows and poplars.

WILLOW
(Salix, several species)

Description
- trees and shrubs, trees often dividing into several main trunks
- buds covered with a single cap-like scale, lying against twig
- twigs, slender, round, smooth
- young bark yellowish, greenish, brown or black depending on species; old bark grey and furrowed

Habitat
- some species common throughout Nova Scotia, wet areas

Notes
- More than 15 species of willows are found in Nova Scotia, all with buds having a single cap-like scale. Identification of species is difficult and will not be attempted in *Nature Notes.* They are most common in wet places, along streams and hillsides where they are important in controlling erosion. Willow trees, which are introduced, and some willow shrubs are planted for ornamental purposes. The young growth provides an important browse for wildlife. The "pussy willows" are the open flower buds which appear in early spring before the leaves.

138

POPLARS

Three species of poplars are native to Nova Scotia and, together with lombardy poplar which is frequently planted, are included in *Nature Notes*. Other types, such as white and silver poplars which are planted as ornamentals, are not included.

All poplars have yellowish-green bark when young, and smooth twigs that are 5 angled (roll between fingers) and have a star-shaped pith. The leaf scars are prominent and raised, triangular in shape, and have three conspicuous bundle scars. The male and female flowers are catkins on separate trees, and develop in spring before the leaves appear.

The four poplars included in *Nature Notes* may be distinguished as follows:

(a) Terminal bud 1 cm or more long, sticky, medicinal odor .... Balsam Poplar

(b) Terminal bud about 0.5 cm long, greyish, hairy .... Large-toothed Aspen

(c) Terminal bud about 0.5 cm long, brown, smooth, tree highly branched and top rounded .... Trembling Aspen

(d) Terminal bud about 0.5 cm long, brown, smooth, branches strongly upcurved forming steeple shape .... Lombardy Poplar

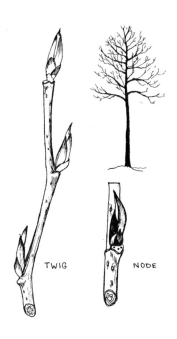

TWIG NODE

BALSAM POPLAR
(Populus balsamifera)

Description
- medium-sized tree
- terminal bud large, 1 cm or more long, reddish-brown, pointed, gummy, fragrant when crushed
- twigs thick, smooth, brown, ridged
- young bark smooth, green-brown; old bark dark and ridged

Habitat
- Cape Breton, valleys, occasionally elsewhere as scattered plantings and escapees

Notes
- Balsam Poplar is native to northern Cape Breton and was once planted elsewhere for ornamental and medicinal purposes. An extract from the buds was used to prepare "Friar's Balsam" which was inhaled during a cold to ease congested breathing.

140

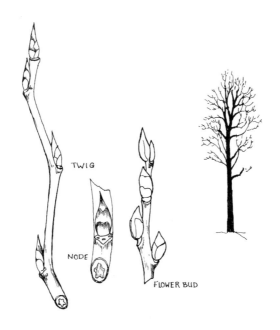

TWIG

NODE

FLOWER BUD

TREMBLING ASPEN
(Populus tremuloides)

Description
- small to medium-sized tree, top rounded
- buds 0.5 cm or less long, pointed, smooth, brown, against twig; leaf buds small, flower buds large
- twig smooth, shiny brown
- young bark smooth and yellowish-green; old bark grey, dark

Habitat
- common throughout Nova Scotia, open sites, often mixed with birches and cherries

Notes
- The Trembling Poplar, Quaking Aspen or Popple, is so-called because the leaf stems are flattened causing the leaves to flutter or tremble in the slightest breeze. The wood has little commercial value other than for pulp and firewood. Poplars reproduce from seeds, as well as by sprouts from roots and cut stumps. They grow rapidly and are important in the initial stages of forest succession, re-establishing quickly in cut, burned, and abandoned areas. They help stabilize the soil and provide shade for the seedlings of other species. Many mammals and birds feed on the twigs and buds of poplar. Beavers prefer poplar, and cut and peeled trees are common around a beaver pond. Beavers feed on the bark, and the branches and trunks are used in the construction of the beaver house and dam.

141

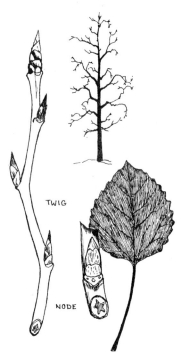

TWIG

NODE

LARGE-TOOTHED ASPEN
(Populus grandidentata)

Description
- medium to large tree, top rounded
- buds about 0.5 cm long, grey, hairy; flower buds large, leaf buds smaller
- twigs grey, slightly hairy
- brown weathered leaves with distinctively large-toothed margins sometimes present on twigs or on ground
- young bark smooth, yellow-green; old bark dark grey or brown

Habitat
- common throughout Nova Scotia, sandy areas
- along streams, hillsides, burned and cut openings

Notes
- Large-toothed Aspen is used for pulp and firewood. Like trembling aspen, its wood is lightweight and is used to make garden furniture. It reproduces rapidly, primarily by seeds and root suckers, and is an early tree along with cherry, birch, and trembling aspen in the re-growth of cut and burned areas. Like trembling aspen, the leaves have a flattened stem and flutter in the slightest breeze. Large-toothed Aspen is an important winter food source for a number of birds and mammals.

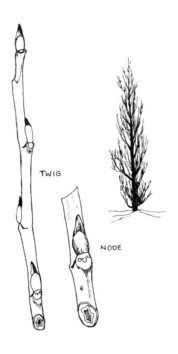

TWIG

NODE

LOMBARDY POPLAR
(Populus nigra)

Description
- medium to large tree, branches upcurved forming steeple-like top
- buds small, 0.5 cm or less long, smooth, yellowish, against twig
- twigs smooth, upcurved, yellowish-green
- young bark yellowish-green, smooth; old bark grey, ridged

Habitat
- planted to form borders

Notes
- Lombardy Poplar is not native to Nova Scotia but was originally imported from Italy. It is a variety developed through the hybridization of black poplar. This hybrid does not produce seeds, and the trees must be reproduced from cuttings. Lombardy Poplar grows rapidly and is planted as a border or wind-break along driveways, and along the edges of property and farm fields. Its upcurved branches and steeple-like shape are unique. It is not a long-lived tree, is susceptible to late spring frosts, and older trees typically contain many dead branches.

143

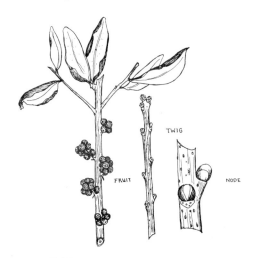

TWIG

FRUIT

NODE

BAYBERRY FAMILY

The bayberry family includes the bayberry, sweet gale and sweet-fern.

BAYBERRY
(Myrica pensylvanica)

Description
- medium height, forming thickets
- leaf scars alternate, crescent-shaped, raised
- lateral buds small, whitish, rounded; terminal bud present
- young twigs at ends of branches, upcurved, greyish-brown, hairy; older branches whitish-grey
- catkin-like flower buds often present, small
- fruit bluish berries covered with whitish wax, clustered along twig
- withered elliptical leaves often present

Habitat
- throughout Nova Scotia: sandy, rocky, gravel and dry areas
- pastures, open woods, coastlines, and valleys

Notes
- The leaves and twigs of Bayberry have a fragrant aroma and are often collected for this scent. Bayberry is also called Candleberry because the wax of the berries, which is extracted by boiling the berries in a small amount of water and filtering through fine cloth to remove the debris, can be used to make candles that burn with a pleasant aroma. When present, the waxy berries provide an identifying characteristic. However, the berries are eaten by many birds, especially the yellow-rumped warbler in the autumn, and are usually not present in winter.

144

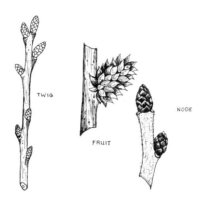

TWIG

NODE

FRUIT

SWEET GALE
(Myrica Gale)

Description
- medium height, forming thickets
- young twigs purplish, smooth, yellowish lenticels, prominent resin droplets
- old branches brown, upcurved
- lateral buds small, conical, whitish; true terminal buds absent
- catkins purplish, clustered at ends of branches
- fruit small, several waxy nuts on short twigs

Habitat
- common throughout Nova Scotia, wet areas
- along streams, lake borders, swamps

Notes
    - Like bayberry, Sweet Gale is an aromatic shrub and its leaves, twigs and berries are collected for their fragrant aroma. Also, the roots of both bayberry and Sweet Gale have nitrogen-fixing bacteria which enrich the soil. Many birds feed on the buds and berries of Sweet Gale and several mammals browse on the foliage and twigs.

145

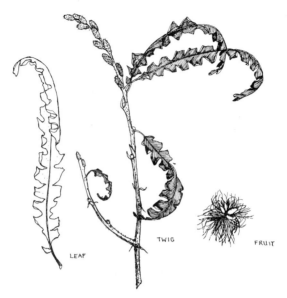

LEAF   TWIG   FRUIT

SWEETFERN
(Myrica asplenifolia)

Description
- low shrub, about 0.5 m or less, branches upcurved, forming thickets
- young twigs yellowish, hairy near ends, droplets of resin present
- old bark brownish, sometimes with yellow or orange tinge
- buds small, withered fern-like leaves sometimes present, aromatic when crushed
- fruit persisting as a burr
- hairy catkins at twig ends

Habitat
- common throughout Nova Scotia; open, dry, often sandy, soil
- pastures, open and rocky woodlands, abandoned fields

Notes
- The leaves and twigs of Sweetfern are fragrant and the odor may persist for some time after cutting. The leaves are elongate and have scalloped borders like the leaves of fern, hence its name. The dried and crushed leaves may be used to make tea, one spoonful per cup of boiling water. The roots contain a type of bacteria which fixes nitrogen, improving the nitrogen content of the soil. The fruit and twigs are eaten by a number of birds and mammals.

146

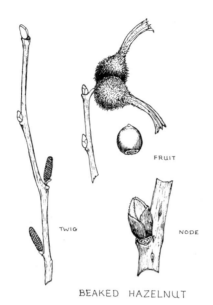

FRUIT

TWIG

NODE

BEAKED HAZELNUT

BIRCH FAMILY

The birch family includes the hazelnut, ironwood, birches, and alders.

BEAKED HAZELNUT
(Corylus cornuta)

Description
- shrubs, branches rooting to form thickets
- twigs smooth, reddish-brown; old bark dark brown
- buds oval, reddish-brown
- male catkins present, about 1 cm long, with sharp scales
- fruit, spherical nut, dark, enclosed in tubular husk

Habitat
- throughout Nova Scotia
- along woodroads, fences, open woods

Notes
- Beaked Hazelnut is so-named because of the tubular husk which encloses the nut. This "beaked" husk is an identifying characterisitic when it is present. It is, however, usually eaten by squirrels, blue jays, or any one of a number of mammals and birds. The nuts ripen in late summer and early autumn. They are edible, very tasty, and may be chopped and added to home-made fudge and cookies.

147

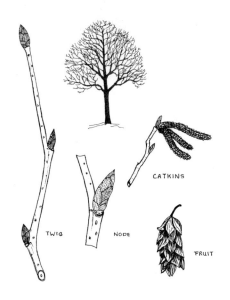

TWIG   NODE   CATKINS   FRUIT

IRONWOOD
(Ostrya virginiana)

Description
- small, slender tree
- buds dark brown, pointed, 3 to 7 mm long
- twigs zig-zagging from bud to bud, red-brown, shiny
- catkins usually present at end of twigs
- bark grey-brown, scaly and curled
- fruit, flat nuts in papery sacs which are clustered and resemble a cone, usually shed in autumn, some remaining into winter

Habitat
- scattered throughout Nova Scotia, not common
- usually an understory tree in hardwoods

Notes
- Ironwood, as it name indicates, has hard, strong wood. The wood may be used to make handles for tools. It is also called hophornbeam because the clusters of papery fruit sacs resemble hops.

148

BIRCHES

Birches have alternating buds, zig-zag shaped twigs, and distinctive bark that is white or yellowish and marked with horizontal lines. The flowers are in the form of catkins. The male catkins form at the end of the twigs in autumn and are present during winter. The female catkins form along the length of the twigs but do not become conspicuous until spring. The fruit is cone-like, about 2 to 4 cm long, and forms along the twig. The cones open during fall and winter and the brown seeds are scattered over the snow. Peeling bark from birch trees will cause the deeper layers to blacken, disfiguring the tree. The three birches that are commonly seen in Nova Scotia may be distinguished as follows:

a) bark yellowish, separating into papery layers
    .... Yellow birch
b) bark white, not separating into papery layers,
    twigs greyish with conspicuous warty pores,
    solitary catkin at end of twig .... Grey birch
c) bark white, separating into papery layers;
    twigs dark brown, pores not conspicuous;
    usually three catkins at end of twig .... White birch

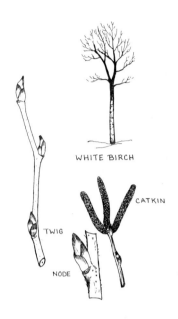

WHITE BIRCH

TWIG

NODE

CATKIN

WHITE BIRCH
(Betula papyrifera)

Description
- medium-sized tree; may be large, ranging up to 20 to 25 m
- twigs dark brown, numerous yellowish or white lenticels
- buds 0.5 cm long, tapering, sticky when pressed between fingers
- catkins, male, usually 3 at end of twig
- bark white, horizontal lines, peeling; bark of saplings reddish-brown with conspicuous lenticels

Habitat
- common throughout Nova Scotia, mixed woods and birch stands
- open areas, abandoned fields, burned and cut areas

Notes
- White Birch, Paper or Canoe Birch, is the tree from which the North American Indian obtained bark for canoes and wigwams. Its wood is easily finished and polished and is used for interior trims and furniture. It is an early tree in forest succession, re-invading abandoned fields, burns, and cut areas, and is later replaced by the shade-casting softwoods. Like other birches, White Birch provides browse for wildlife and seeds and buds which are eaten by many species of birds.

150

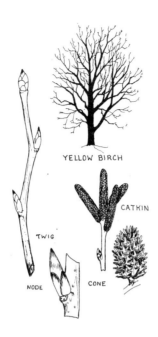

YELLOW BIRCH

CATKIN

TWIG

NODE

CONE

YELLOW BIRCH
(Betula lutea)

Description
- medium-sized, sometimes large, tree
- twigs brown, distinct wintergreen taste and odor when crushed
- male catkins, usually 3 or 4 near end of twig
- buds hairy or scaly, not sticky
- small cones often present in winter
- young bark yellowish, horizontal lenticels, peeling into small curls; old bark dark brown or black, flaking

Habitat
- common throughout Nova Scotia, mixed woods
- borders of lakes and swamps, hillsides

Notes
- Yellow Birch may become a very old tree, reaching a metre in diameter and having a broad, fully branched crown. Such old trees are occasionally found in Nova Scotian woodlands. Its wood is used for interior finishings and furniture. Oil of wintergreen may be extracted from its bark and leaves. Yellow Birch is browsed by deer, moose and rabbits. Many species of birds feed on the seeds, buds and catkins.

151

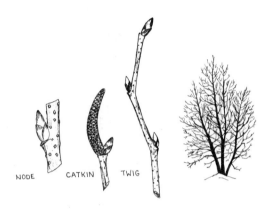

NODE   CATKIN   TWIG

GREY BIRCH
(Betula populifolia)

Description
- small tree, trunks single or clumped and shrub-like
- older bark white, black areas below branches or marking sites of former branches, usually not peeling
- twigs slender, grey or red-brown, warty pores prominent, usually a single male catkin near twig end
- buds short, spindle-shaped, sticky

Habitat
- common throughout Nova Scotia, open sites
- bordering swamps, abandoned fields and pastures, burned and cut areas

Notes
- The Grey Birch, or Wire Birch, is used for firewood but otherwise is too small to be of commercial value. It appears early in forest succession, re-populating abandoned fields, cut areas and crowding into swamps. It is soon replaced by pine and other hardwoods. It provides browse for wildlife, and seeds and buds for many species of birds.

152

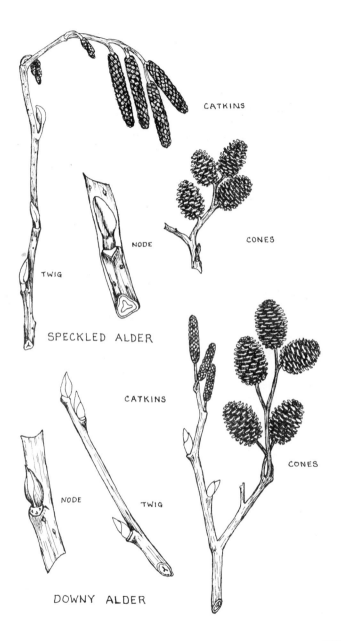

CATKINS

CONES

NODE

TWIG

SPECKLED ALDER

CATKINS

NODE

TWIG

CONES

DOWNY ALDER

153

SPECKLED ALDER DOWNY OR GREEN ALDER
(Alnus rugosa) *(Alnus crispa)*

Several species and varieties of alders occur in Nova Scotia. Of these, the Speckled and Downy Alders are the most common.

Description
- open shrubs or small trees, growing in extensive thickets, main branches form close to ground
- leaf scars semi-circular, 3 bundle scars
- elongate staminate (male) catkins for coming season present in winter
- woody cones, from previous season, persisting through winter, 1 to 2 cm long
- pith triangular

Speckled Alder
- bark "speckled" with white, raised lenticels; buds stalked; seeds small, spherical nuts; catkins hanging

Downy Alder
- bark not marked; buds not stalked; seeds small, winged nuts, often seen on the snow; catkins erect

Habitat
- both species common throughout Nova Scotia
- speckled alder in wet areas, pastures, banks of streams, swamps
- downy alder in drier areas, hillsides, more common near coast

Notes
- Alders represent an early stage in forest succession, reinvading deserted fields, pastures, swamps, etc. Their roots contain nitrogen-fixing bacteria and they improve the nitrogen content of the soil. Many birds, for example grouse, feed on alder buds and fruit. Woodpeckers are often present in alder thickets. Many seed-eating birds, goldfinches, juncos, and sparrows, are frequently seen on the snow feeding on the nuts under alder bushes. Mammals, such as rabbits, muskrats, and deer browse on the twigs. Rabbits may be especially plentiful in alder thickets and their tracks are frequently seen in the snow.

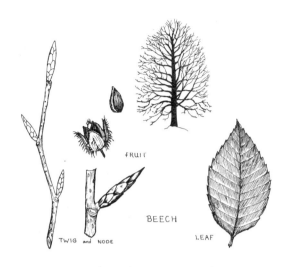

FRUIT

BEECH

TWIG and NODE

LEAF

BEECH FAMILY

The beech family includes the beech and the oak trees.

BEECH
(Fagus grandifolia)

Description
- medium-sized, sometimes large, tree
- buds 1 to 2 cm or more long, slender and pointed, standing out from twig
- twigs long, forming zig-zag pattern, brown
- bark smooth and grey, often showing light and dark areas
- fruit prickly, often paired, containing 1 or 2 brown nuts; shed in autumn but opened husks may remain on tree into winter
- leaves may persist on trees, especially young trees, into winter; dried leaves elliptical, up to 12 cm or more in length, toothed, distinctively straight veined.

Habitat
- common throughout Nova Scotia, often on hillsides
- pure or mixed stands

Notes
- Beech is used for firewood and may often be planted as an ornamental. Beech nuts are shed in autumn and are sweet and edible either raw or roasted. The nuts are produced in large numbers about every three years. The twigs and fruit are eaten by many species of mammals and birds. Beech trees often show extensive areas of abnormal growth called cankers. These develop following a fungus infection which invades sites of injury caused by accident or insect attack.

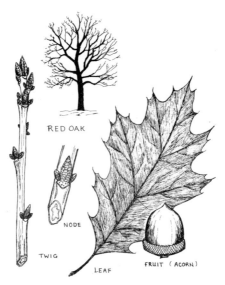

RED OAK

TWIG

NODE

LEAF

FRUIT (ACORN)

RED OAK
(Quercus borealis)

Description
- large tree
- buds reddish-brown, 0.5 cm long, smooth, clustered at twig end
- twigs slender and smooth, 5-sided (roll between fingers), star-shaped pith
- young bark smooth; old bark dark, flat ridges
- acorns present, about as wide as long, 1 to 3 cm long, about 1/3 of acorn covered with cap, mature during second year and present on tree overwinter
- dried leaves may remain on tree for much of the winter or are present on ground; leaves elongate, deeply lobed, lobes pointed

Habitat
- scattered throughout Nova Scotia, sand and gravel areas
- mixed woods, ornamentals

Notes
- Oak wood is brownish and is used for interior finishings and furniture. Red Oak is often planted as a shade tree. Other oaks, such as English Oak, have been imported for ornamentals, have spread along roadsides, and may be locally common. (The acorns of English Oak mature in the first year and, unlike Red Oak, are not present on the tree over winter. Also, the leaves of the English Oak have rounded and not pointed lobes.) The nuts can be roasted and eaten, after boiling in water to remove excess tanin (a yellowish-brown dye) which gives a bitter taste. The acorns are eaten by many birds and mammals, and are favourites of blue jays, grouse, squirrels and deer.

156

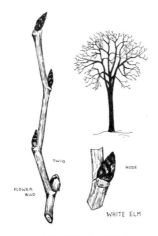

TWIG

NODE

FLOWER
BUD

WHITE ELM

ELM FAMILY
WHITE ELM
(Ulmus americana)

Description
- large tree, characterisitc "vase" shape when grown in open
- twigs smooth, reddish-brown, small branches rough
- buds reddish-brown, 2 to 3 mm long, end bud placed to one side of twig end, flower buds larger than leaf bud, bud scales bordered in black
- young bark reddish-brown; old bark grey-brown, furrowed

Habitat
- scattered throughout Nova Scotia, especially valleys
- commonly planted in towns, mixed with hardwoods in woodlands

Notes
- White Elm, or American Elm, is often planted as an ornamental because of its shape, rapid growth, and long life. Older elms may reach well over 30 metres in height and more than one metre in diameter. Several other elms have been introduced for ornamental purposes. They are found only in towns and not in the woodlands. Elms are endangered by Dutch elm disease. This fungus blocks the vessels in the tree, preventing water and minerals from rising to the branches and leaves. This results in wilting, yellowing, and death first of the crown branches and later of the entire tree. The fungus is carried by the elm bark beetle, and one control is to burn or bury the dead and dying wood and thereby eliminate breeding sites for the beetles. Orioles build their nests in elm trees during summer. In winter these hanging nests may be seen swinging from the ends of the branches.

157

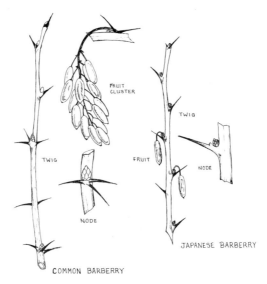

FRUIT CLUSTER

TWIG

TWIG

FRUIT

NODE

NODE

JAPANESE BARBERRY

COMMON BARBERRY

BARBERRY FAMILY

JAPANESE BARBERRY
(Berberis thunbergii)

Description
- upright shrub, medium height, branches arched, forming thickets
- twigs grooved, brown, yellow wood and pith
- buds small
- thorns present, single
- fruit: red berries, round or elliptical, may persist into winter

Habitat
- throughout Nova Scotia, planted about homes and escaping from cultivation
- in wild: old pastures, deserted gardens, roadsides

Notes
- Japanese Barberry is planted as an ornamental and to form hedges. It is a common escapee. The common barberry (*Barberis vulgaris*), once frequently planted, can be distinguished from Japanese barberry because many of its thorns are divided into 3 branches of equal length. Common Barberry is an alternate host for rusts of wheat and much of it has been destroyed. The Japanese barberry and the other varieties which are now imported are not hosts to the wheat rusts. Many birds, including grouse and pheasant, feed on the berries. A yellow dye can be boiled out of the stems and roots and used to color clothing and wood. The berries may be used to make jam.

158

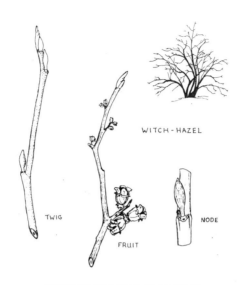

TWIG

WITCH-HAZEL

FRUIT

NODE

WITCH-HAZEL FAMILY

The witch-hazel is the only member of this family in Nova Scotia.

WITCH-HAZEL
(Hamamelis virginiana)

Description
- small tree, crooked, frequently clustered shrubs
- buds yellow-brown, no bud scales, hairy; two end buds, lateral buds stalked
- twigs orange-brown, hairy, young pith greenish, empty fruit capsules persisting into winter
- young bark smooth, brown; old bark scaly; warty cross-markings

Habitat
- scattered throughout Nova Scotia, more common in central part of province, not in Cape Breton
- wet woods, rocky habitats, areas of young growth

Notes
- Witch-Hazel is also called Winter Bloom because it blooms in autumn after its leaves have fallen and its yellow flowers remain on the shrub into early winter. The fruit takes one year to ripen and the fruit capsules are still present when the flowers in the following autumn bloom. The fruit capsule snaps open shooting the two black nuts several metres. Forked branches of Witch-Hazel are used by water diviners to search for underground water.

159

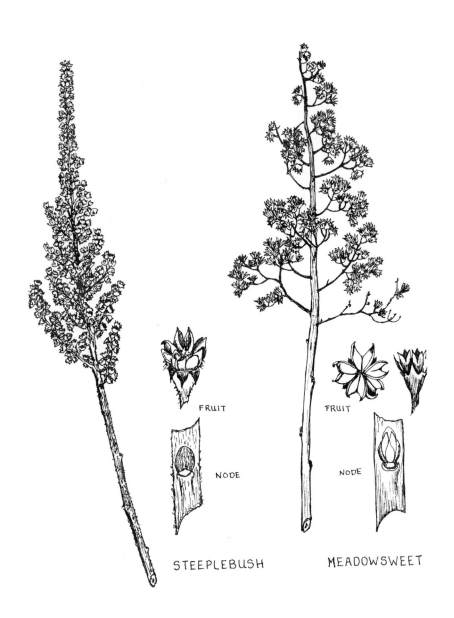

FRUIT

NODE

STEEPLEBUSH

FRUIT

NODE

MEADOWSWEET

ROSE FAMILY

The rose family is a large family of trees, shrubs, and herbaceous plants. Members of this family in *Nature Notes* are: spirea, apple, chokeberry, mountain ash, shadbush, hawthorne, raspberry, blackberry, dewberry, rose, and cherry.

SPIREAS

MEADOWSWEET, WHITE HARDHACK
(Spirea latifolia)
STEEPLEBUSH, RED HARDHACK
(Spirea tomentosa)

Description
- erect shrubs, about 1 m or less high, little branched, forming thickets
- stems slender, wand-like, ends often winter-killed
- buds small, leaf scars raised and crescent-shaped
- outer bark papery, peeling
- clusters of dried flowers and fruit common at twig ends

Meadowsweet - young twigs smooth, reddish, old flower clusters branched and wide

Steeplebush - young twigs wooly, rusty colored, old flower clusters straight and narrow

Habitat
- both species common throughout Nova Scotia
- both species in moist areas, roadsides, ditches, wet meadows and pastures

Notes
- The Spireas are well known for their flowers, both flowering during summer. Those of Meadowsweet are white and those of Steeplebush are pink. Several cultivated Spireas are also planted about homes for decorative purposes. The buds and seeds are eaten by several species of birds and the twigs are browsed by a number of mammals.

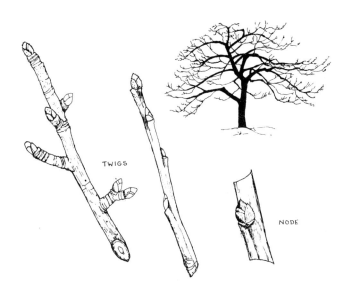

TWIGS

NODE

APPLE
(Pyrus malus)

Description
- small tree, short trunk with several low branches, rounded shape
- buds oval, reddish-grey, wooly
- twigs wooly with sweet taste, buds crowded on spur branches
- young bark brown with reddish or greenish tinge; old bark grey, scaly

Habitat
- cultivated in orchards, planted about homes
- escaped into woodlands near abandoned farms

Notes
- Eating apples and crabapples are planted both for fruit and ornamental purposes. The cultivated varieties have been developed through hybridization from stock originally imported from Europe. These cultivated hybrids must be maintained through graftings, planting seeds results in many varieties which reflect the history of the stock. The buds and fruit grow on spur branches. Spur branches grow very slowly and show several annual rings which are close together. Apple trees, wild and cultivated, are popular feeding spots for many birds and mammals, especially robins, grosbeaks, raccoons, and deer.

162

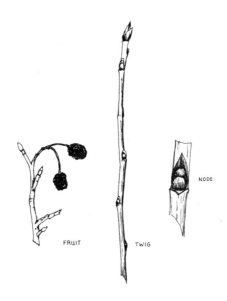

FRUIT   TWIG   NODE

CHOKEBERRY
(Aronia 3 species)

Description
- medium-sized shrub, often forming thickets
- buds 0.5 cm long, dark red, smooth, pointed, against twig, tip of bud scales notched (use hand lens)
- twigs grey, often hairy
- leaf scars alternate, V-shaped

Habitat
- throughout Nova Scotia, wet and dry sites
- swamps, lake shores, gravel and sandy areas

Notes

- There are three species of Chokeberry in Nova Scotia, Red Chokeberry, Purple Chokeberry, and Black Chokeberry, so-named because of the colour of their berries. The three are difficult to distinguish in the winter when the berries are absent, although the berries of Black Chokeberry may remain. The fruit is eaten by pheasants, partridge, and a variety of seed-eating birds. The berries have a high pectin content and may be used to stiffen jelly. Do not confuse chokeberry with the entirely different choke cherry.

163

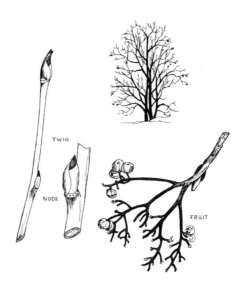

MOUNTAIN ASH
(Sorbus americana)

Description
- small tree, short trunk, dividing into several branches, may be shrub-like
- buds dark, smooth or slightly hairy, may be sticky; terminal bud large, 2 cm long; lateral buds smaller, against stem
- twigs reddish-brown or grey, smooth, horizontal white lenticels prominent; pith round and brownish; leaf scars narrow on raised swellings
- young bark smooth, grey or grey-green; old bark grey, brownish, scaly

Habitat
- throughout Nova Scotia, ornamentals near homes
- open areas in woodlands, roadsides

Notes
- Mountain ash is native to Nova Scotia and is common throughout the province. Two other species are also present. The Dogberry is native but less common, and is difficult to distinguish from Mountain Ash in winter. The Rowan tree is imported and planted for its ornamental value and to attract birds. It has spread along the roadsides. The Rowan tree can be distinguished from the other two by its buds, which are whitish and more wooly than the native species. The fruits of all three species are clusters of red berries which may remain into winter but which are usually quickly eaten by birds, especially robins, waxwings and starlings.

164

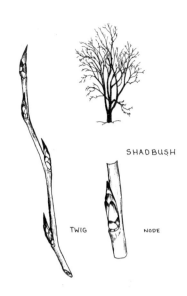

SHADBUSH

TWIG   NODE

SHADBUSH, SERVICEBERRIES
(Amelanchier, several species)

Description
- small trees and shrubs
- buds 1 to 2 cm long, greenish or purplish-brown, pointed, lying along twig (not standing out as in beech); numerous overlapping scales with black tips
- twigs slender, pith 5-sided; lenticels white, elongate, conspicuous
- young bark smooth, grey marked with reddish-brown; old bark scaly

Habitat
- some species common throughout Nova Scotia
- open areas along streams, swamps, roadsides, woodland clearings

Notes
- There are a number of species of Shadbush, Juneberries, Wild or Indian Pear, and Serviceberries in Nova Scotia. They are among the first woodland trees and shrubs to bloom in spring when they give magnificent displays of white flowers before the leaves are fully formed. They are called "Shadbush" because they bloom when the shad are moving into the rivers. They are found in open areas mixed with cherries from which they can be distinguished by their larger buds. The berries may be collected in autumn, dried or preserved, and used in cooking. The fruit are eaten by a number of mammals and birds, and the twigs are browsed by several mammals.

165

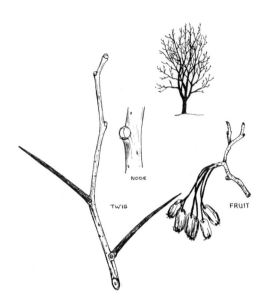

NODE

TWIG

FRUIT

HAWTHORNES
(Crataegus, several species)

Description
- small or medium-sized trees; shrubs, often forming thickets
- thorns, sharp, 1 to 5 cm long, unbranched
- buds reddish-brown, small
- twigs smooth
- young bark grey; old bark brownish and flaking
- fruit red, fleshy

Habitat
- some species common throughout Nova Scotia, open and sunny sites
- along streams and lakes, roads, hedges, abandoned fields

Notes
- The two Hawthornes that reach tree size in Nova Scotia are the American Hawthorne (fruit contains several seeds and the thorns grow directly from the twigs) and the introduced and often escaping English Hawthorne (fruit contains one seed and the thorns grow on small, spur branches). The other types of Hawthornes are shrubs. The fruit is eaten by many birds and mammals. Hawthornes are often planted as ornamentals for their spring flower display and for their fruit to attract winter birds. Hawthornes spread rapidly into abandoned fields where the seeds are dispersed by birds and small mammals.

166

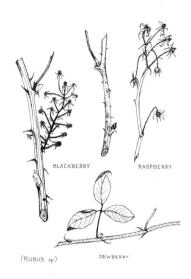

BLACKBERRY   RASPBERRY

(RUBUS sp)   DEWBERRY

RASPBERRIES, BLACKBERRIES, DEWBERRIES
(Rubus, many species and varieties)

Description
- shrubs forming extensive thickets
- stems or canes upright, arching, greenish or reddish, armed with fine stiff bristles and sharp prickles, large pith
- stems biennial, fruiting and dying in second season, many dead canes within thicket, new canes shoot from root
- outer bark of old canes shredding in some species
- buds oval, medium sized
- in many species, blade of leaf is lost in autumn but the stem of the leaf persists attached to cane through winter
- remains of inflorescences persisting

Habitat
- some species common throughout Nova Scotia
- many species prefer dry, open habitats; thickets along roadsides, abandoned fields, woodland burns and clearings
- other species prefer moist habitats; along streams, edges of ponds

Notes
- Many species of Raspberries, Blackberries and Dewberries are found in Nova Scotia. Some are native, others are introduced for cultivation and often escape around abandoned farms and gardens. Raspberries have round stems and erect, arching canes. Blackberries have angular stems and erect, arching canes. The canes of Dewberry are prostrate and trailing. The berries are edible and are used to make jelly and jam. Raspberries, Blackberries and Dewberries, together with roses, make up a group of plants that are often referred to as brambles. Brambles provide an important cover and food source for wildlife.

167

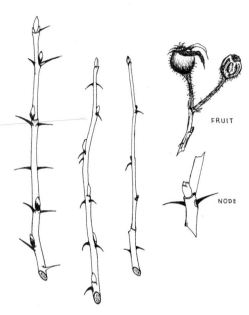

FRUIT

NODE

ROSE
(Rosa, several species*)*

Description
- arching shrubs, may climb trees or brush piles, forming briar thickets
- twigs slender, red or green, stiff prickles or decurved thorns
- leaf scars narrow (line-like), half encircling twig
- buds small
- pith large, brown
- fruit fleshy, red hip, remaining on shrub into winter

Habitat
- some species common throughout Nova Scotia, various habitats
- some species escaping around old farms, gardens, pastures, roadsides
- other species in wet habitats, around swamps, marshes

Notes
- About 9 species of rose, with hybrids occurring between some, occur in the wild state in Nova Scotia. Rose thickets provide good cover for wildlife and the fleshy fruit provides a winter food for a number of birds and animals. In particular, rose hips are a favourite food for pheasants and grouse, wintering robins, and that occasional winter visitor, the mockingbird. The floribunda varieties, often planted as hedges, attract large numbers of birds. Rose hips may be used to make jam and jelly, eaten fresh, or sliced into a salad. They are an excellent dietary source of vitamin C, calcium and iron.

168

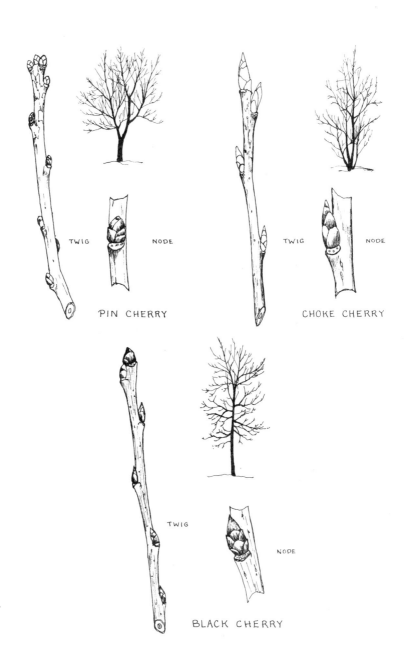

TWIG   NODE

PIN CHERRY

TWIG   NODE

CHOKE CHERRY

TWIG

NODE

BLACK CHERRY

CHERRIES

The genus *Prunus* includes the cherries, plums, and peaches. A number of varieties are planted domestically for fruit or as ornamentals, and escapees from these plantings are locally common about towns, abandoned farms and roadsides. Three species of cherries are native and common in our woodlands, and they are the only ones included in *Nature Notes*. All are trees or shrubs with smooth dark bark showing a reddish tinge and marked with horizontal lenticels. The buds are small, less than 0.5 cm long, and in alternating positions along the twig. The twigs have semi-circular leaf scars and a bitter almond taste. A centrally placed terminal bud is present in cherries but is either lacking or placed to one side of the twig tip in plums and peaches. Unlike birches, cherry twigs are straight and there are no catkins. Our three woodland cherries may be distinguished as follows:

1. Buds clustered at ends of twig .... Pin Cherry

2. Buds not clustered, buds about 5 mm long with rounded scales, twigs grey-brown and dull ... Choke Cherry

3. Buds not clustered, buds about 3 mm long with pointed scales, twigs red-brown and glossy .... Black Cherry

PIN CHERRY
(Prunus pensylvanica)

Description
- small tree, may be shrub-like
- buds small (smallest of any tree in Nova Scotia), clustered at end of twig, round, reddish-brown, often on spur twigs
- twigs smooth, reddish, peeling skin
- young bark smooth, reddish, yellowish lenticels; old bark dark red-brown with thin outer layers peeling and exposing green inner layers
- black knot fungus often on branches

Habitat
- very common throughout Nova Scotia; open, not shady, areas
- roadsides, borders of fields and pastures, cut and burned openings, margins of woods, etc.

Notes
- The Pin Cherry was so-named because its fruit, red cherries on long stems, looks like a cluster of large-headed pins. It is also called fire cherry because it is one of the first trees to become re-established in cut or burned areas or in abandoned fields. In these early stages of forest succession, it limits erosion and provides shade permitting other trees to develop. It is, in turn, overgrown, shaded, and replaced by conifers. The tree is not large enough to be of commercial value. The cherries may be used to make jelly, and the fruit, buds and twigs
170

provide an important food source for wildlife. Robins, starlings, and purple finches are frequently seen feeding on pin cherries.

CHOKE CHERRY
(Prunus virginiana)

Description
- small trees, shrubs, often forming thickets
- buds pointed, 0.5 cm or less long, brown, rounded scales, not clustered
- twigs and bark smooth, grey-brown, not peeling, lenticels not conspicuous, black knot fungus often on branches; old bark scaly

Habitat
- common throughout Nova Scotia, moist and open areas
- roadsides, borders of fields and pastures, cut and burned openings, margins of woods, along lakes and streams, etc.

Notes
- The fruit of Choke Cherry may be used to make jelly and wine. Like pin cherry, it is one of the first trees to re-establish in areas opened by cutting or fire and is, in turn, overgrown, shaded, and replaced by conifers. The cherries are eaten by wild birds and mammals, but the foliage and twigs may be toxic to domestic animals.

BLACK CHERRY
(Prunus serotina)

Description
- small to medium-sized tree
- buds about 3 mm or less long, pointed, chestnut colored, pointed scales, shiny, not clustered
- twigs reddish-brown, often peeling
- young bark reddish-brown, shiny; lenticels white, horizontal lines; old bark dark, flaking, underbark reddish

Habitat
- common throughout much of mainland Nova Scotia, less common in eastern counties, not in Cape Breton
- moist soils, along streams and lakes, ravines, in mixed hardwoods

Notes
- The wood of Black Cherry is reddish-brown, is easily finished and polished, and is highly valued for making furniture and interior finishings. The cherries may be used to make jelly and wine. Wild mammals browse on this tree and many birds eat the cherries. Like choke cherry, the twigs and foliage may be toxic to domestic animals.

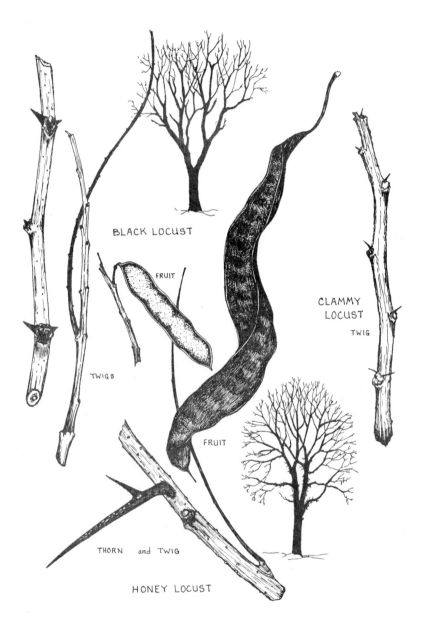

BLACK LOCUST

FRUIT

TWIGS

CLAMMY
LOCUST

TWIG

FRUIT

THORN and TWIG

HONEY LOCUST

LEGUME FAMILY

The legume family includes all plants that produce fruit in a pod, such as the well-know peas and beans. Locust trees belong to the legume family and produce pod fruit. Three species of locusts have been introduced to Nova Scotia: Honey Locust, Black Locust, and Clammy Locust (or Rose Acacia).

HONEY LOCUST
(Gleditsia triacanthos)

BLACK LOCUST
(Robina pseudo-acacia)

CLAMMY LOCUST
(Robina viscosa)

Descriptions:

- All three
- buds covered with leaf scar, no end-bud, spines or thorns present
- Honey Locust
- medium to large tree
- thorns long, single or branched, between nodes
- fruit, large pod (4 dm long), usually falling before winter
- young bark smooth, prominent lenticels, old bark plated
- Black Locust
- medium to large tree
- thorns short, on either side of leaf scar
- fruit, short pods (5-10 cm long), often on trees in winter
- twigs greenish or reddish, smooth, angular
- old bark distinctively thick-ridged with deep furrows
- Clammy Locust
- small trees, shrubs, forming thickets
- thorns short, on either side of leaf scar
- twigs sticky or clammy
- no fruit pods

Habitat
- plantings in many parts of province
- more common in central counties and Annapolis Valley

Notes
- Locusts have been introduced to Nova Scotia from the central and eastern United States. The Black and Clammy Locusts produce white and rose coloured, highly fragrant, flowers. Some locust trees and thickets are the result of very old plantings where the stand has been maintained through growth of new trees and shrubs from the roots of older trees. Locusts are found around homes, on town streets and escaping along roadsides, and in abandoned areas where they mark the sites of earlier homesteads.

173

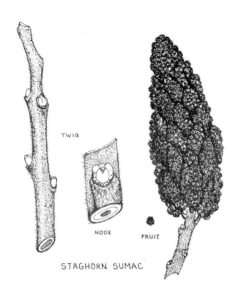

TWIG

NODE

FRUIT

STAGHORN SUMAC

SUMAC FAMILY

STAGHORN SUMAC
(Rhus typhina)

Description
- large shrubs, open and erect; forming thickets with flat or evenly rounded tops
- leaf scars horse-shoe shaped, encircling small lateral bud
- twigs thick, brown, densely hairy; older bark smooth, raised lenticels; tips often dead
- pith large, yellowish
- fruit, densely clustered berries, red, hairy, terminal on branch, persisting into winter

Habitat
- throughout Nova Scotia; open, dry habitats
- roadsides, abandoned fields, borders and fences

Notes
- Staghorn Sumac is so-named because the erect branches covered with dense, brown hair resemble the velvet-covered horns of a stag deer. The fruit remains into winter and is eaten by a number of birds, including grouse and evening grosbeaks. Deer, rabbits and other wildlife may eat the twigs but signs of browsing are not common suggesting that it is not a preferred food. Sumac lemonade may be made from the berries. Steep crushed berries in boiled water while it cools, filter to remove debris, sweeten, and drink hot or cold. Berries collected in autumn or early winter may be used, but those exposed to the winter and gathered in spring make the most tasty drink.

174

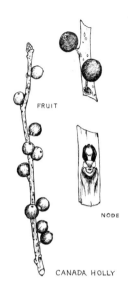

FRUIT

NODE

CANADA HOLLY

HOLLY FAMILY

Three hollies, all shrubs, are present in Nova Scotia. Canada holly and false holly are included in *Nature Notes.*

CANADA HOLLY
(Ilex verticillata)

Description
- tall shrub, up to 3 to 4 m, upcurved branches
- buds small, rounded, grey or brown
- young bark ash-grey; old bark smooth
- twigs angular; leaf scars narrow, sometimes crowded on spur twigs
- fruit red, 0.5 cm in diameter, usually in clusters of 2 or 3 berries, against twig

Habitat
- throughout Nova Scotia; usually wet woods, swamps, open habitats

Notes
- Canada Holly, or winterberry, bears clusters of red berries which are collected for Christmas decorations. Berries will not be found on all shrubs since the male and female flowers occur on different plants. The berries form in early autmn and remain on the shrub into winter after the leaves have fallen.

175

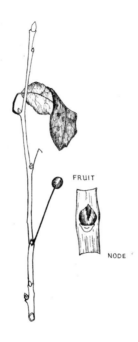

FRUIT

NODE

MOUNTAIN HOLLY
(Nemopanthus mucronata)

Description
- highly branched shrub, up to 3 m in height
- young twigs purplish with a bluish-white bloom which can be rubbed off; old branches ash-grey
- leaf scars small, crescent-shaped, 1 bundle scar
- buds small, pointed, clustered at twig ends or on small spur branches
- fruit red, long stems, 0.5 cm diameter, may persist into winter

Habitat
- throughout Nova Scotia, less common near coast
- wet habitats, lake borders, swamps, bogs

Notes
- Mountain Holly, or False Holly, produces red berries in early autumn which may persist into winter. The twigs and berries may be collected and dried for Christmas decorations.

176

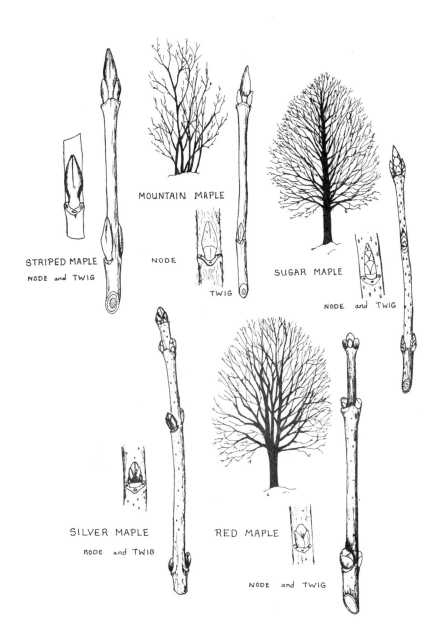

STRIPED MAPLE
NODE and TWIG

MOUNTAIN MAPLE

NODE

TWIG

SUGAR MAPLE

NODE and TWIG

SILVER MAPLE

NODE and TWIG

RED MAPLE

NODE and TWIG

177

MAPLE FAMILY

Maples form a conspicuous feature of the woodlands in autumn when their leaves turn red, gold, and yellow. In winter, maples can be distinguished by their smooth, reddish or brownish buds which are arranged opposite to one another. Five species of maples are commonly found in the woodlands or along the highways of Nova Scotia. Others, such as Norway maple and Manitoba maple, are frequently planted as ornamentals but are not found in the woodlands and are not included in these *Nature Notes*. The maples may be distinguished with the following guide:

a)   Buds stalked, terminal bud about 1 cm long, young twigs and buds smooth and red, older bark green or brown and distinctly striped .... Striped Maple

b)   Buds stalked, terminal bud 0.5 cm or less long, buds and young twigs purplish, older bark greenish but not striped .... Mountain Maple

c)   Buds not stalked, brown, slender, pointed .. Sugar Maple

d)   Buds not stalked, oval, reddish, crushed twigs with unpleasant odor, old bark flaking .... Silver Maple

e)   Buds not stalked, oval, reddish, crushed twigs without unpleasant odor, old bark not flaking .... Red Maple

STRIPED MAPLE
(Acer pensylvanicum)

Description
- small tree, highly branched, may be shrub-like
- buds stalked, red, covered with 2 visible scales, smooth, terminal bud about 1 cm long
- twigs smooth, young growth red
- bark greenish or brown, conspicuous white or yellowish vertical stripes

Habitat
- throughout Nova Scotia, shaded and damp woods
- borders of streams and lakes, ditches, undergrowth in mixed woods

Notes
- Striped Maple is also called Moose Maple because it provides an important browse for moose and deer, as well as food for birds and other wildlife. It is too small to be of commercial value.

178

MOUNTAIN MAPLE
(Acer spicatum)

Description
- small tree, highly branched, may be shrub-like
- buds stalked, red, covered with 2 visible scales, finely hairy, terminal bud 0.5 cm or less long
- twigs purplish, finely hairy near tip, white lenticels
- young bark smooth, reddish, green or grey; old bark grey, no vertical stripes

Habitat
- throughout Nova Scotia, more common at higher elevations, shaded and wet sites
- borders of streams and lakes, ditches, undergrowth in mixed woods

Notes
- Mountain Maple is an important food source for wildlife. Moose and deer browse the twigs, and several types of birds feed on the buds and seeds.

SUGAR MAPLE
(Acer saccharum)

Description
- medium to large tree, crown rounded and highly branched
- buds 1 cm or less long, pointed, brown, covered with several scales
- twigs smooth, shiny, brown, dotted with yellow or white lenticels
- young bark grey-brown, smooth; old bark dark, grey-brown, thick scales

Habitat
- common throughout Nova Scotia
- mixed woodlands, planted along streets

Notes
- Sugar Maple, or Rock Maple has a hard brownish wood which takes a good finish. It is used for interior finishing and furniture. The "Curly" or "Bird's-Eye" grains used in making furniture are obtained from abnormal growth patterns of the Sugar Maple. The sap of Sugar Maple is collected in spring to make syrup and maple syrup. The tree may live for more than 200 years and will grow to about 1 m in diameter. Its seeds are an important food for a number of bird species, such as evening and pine grosbeaks, and several mammals browse on the twigs.

SILVER MAPLE
(Acer saccharinum)

Description
- medium to large tree, crown rounded and highly branched
- buds 0.5 cm or less long, oval, reddish, clustered, covered with several scales
- twigs smooth, reddish-brown, have unpleasant odor when crushed
- young bark smooth and reddish-grey; old bark dark grey, furrowed and scaly

Habitat
- planted about homes and along streets, escaping along roadsides and borders of fields, not in deep woodlands

Notes

- The Silver Maple is not native to Nova Scotia but is frequently planted as an ornamental. It is native to New Brunswick. It may grow to heights of over 30 m and to diameters of over 1 m. The wood is not as hard as that of sugar maple but may be used for furniture and interior finishing.

RED MAPLE
(Acer rubrum)

Description
- medium to large tree, may be shrub-like in cut openings
- buds less than 0.5 cm long, rounded, red, covered with several scales
- twigs smooth, red, white lenticels
- young bark grey; old bark dark, scaly

Habitat
- common throughout Nova Scotia
- swamps, rocky woodlands, cut and burned openings

Notes

- Red Maple, Scarlet Maple, or Swamp Maple, is the most common maple in Nova Scotia. It grows throughout the woodlands and is also planted as an ornamental. This is the maple with the bright scarlet leaves in autumn. On good soils it may reach 30 m in height and more than 1 m in diameter. In rocky woodlands the tree remains small. The wood is used for furniture and interior finishing and the smaller trees provide fuel wood. Like other maples, Red Maple is an important food source for wildlife.

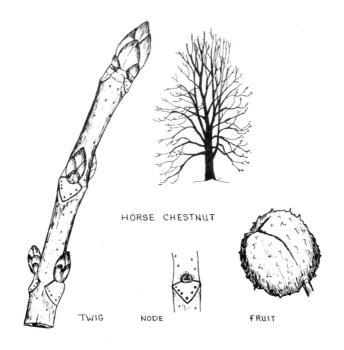

HORSE CHESTNUT

TWIG   NODE   FRUIT

HORSE CHESTNUT FAMILY

No member of this family is native to Nova Scotia. The horse chestnut is frequently planted as an ornamental.

HORSE CHESTNUT
(Aesculus hippocastanum)

Description
- usually medium-sized tree, many branches, rounded top
- buds large, oval, chestnut-colored, sticky, shiny
- twigs stout, conspicuous leaf scars shaped like a horse shoe with bundle scars resembling shoe nails
- young bark brown and smooth; old bark fissured and scaly

Habitat
- planted near homes, not in deep woods

Notes
- The Horse Chestnut is imported from Europe. It is planted as a shade tree and for its flowers in the springtime. Its fruit is the well-known chestnut, one to three shiny reddish-brown nuts encased in a thick prickly husk. The nuts of this chestnut are not edible. Nuts and husks can usually be found under the tree in winter.

181

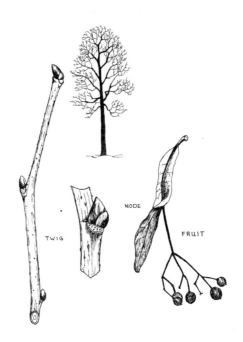

TWIG   NODE   FRUIT

LINDEN FAMILY

No member of the linden family is native to Nova Scotia. Basswood is planted as an ornamental.

BASSWOOD
(Tilia europea)

Description
- medium to large tree
- twigs smooth, brownish
- larger buds red or greenish, covered with 2 or 3 scales, rounded, 0.5 cm or less long, asymmetrical in shape, standing out from twig, end bud to one side of twig tip
- fruit clusters are characteristic if present, nut-like berries attached to leaf-like blade, shed in autumn and early winter but many persisting on tree for some time into winter
- young bark smooth, grey; old bark dark, furrowed

Habitat
- planted near homes, along town streets, not in woodlands

Notes
- Basswood, or Linden, is not native to Nova Scotia but is commonly planted as a shade tree and for its flowers. It has spread along roadsides. The wood is soft, light, and straight grained and is popular for wood carving.

182

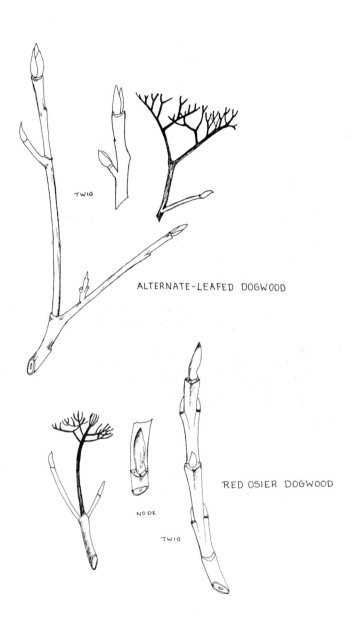

TWIG

ALTERNATE-LEAFED DOGWOOD

RED OSIER DOGWOOD

NODE

TWIG

183

DOGWOOD FAMILY

Several species of dogwood are present in Nova Scotia. The red osier and the alternate-leaved dogwoods are shrub size and are frequently found.

RED OSIER DOGWOOD
(Cornus stolonifera)
ALTERNATE-LEAVED DOGWOOD
(Cornus alternifolia)

Description

Red Osier Dogwood
- shrub, less than 2 m high, central branches straight and erect
- leaf scars opposite, thin and crescent-shaped
- branches and twigs red, smooth; buds small

Alternate-leaved Dogwood
- tall erect shrub or small tree
- leaf scars alternate, crowded near ends of twigs as if whorled, narrow and crescent-shaped, raised on new growth
- twigs greenish, reddish, may be streaked with white; buds small

Habitat
-Alternate-leaved Dogwood throughout Nova Scotia
- Red Osier Dogwood more common in Annapolis Valley and adjacent North Mountain, central counties and Cape Breton
- open woodlands, near streams and meadows

Notes
-Dogwood is browsed by several mammals and the fruit is eaten by several species of birds. Dogwoods are often planted as ornamentals for their flowers and to attract birds. Red Osier is a popular ornamental because of its red bark which gives a brilliant contrast with the snow. Red Osier often forms dense thickets by spreading underground and by the rooting of the drooping branches. These branches root like stolons, hence their scientific species name.

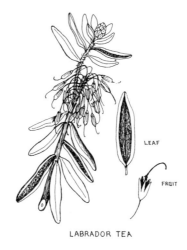

LEAF

FRUIT

LABRADOR TEA

HEATH FAMILY

The heath family is a large family of low shrubs. The species included in *Nature Notes* are Labrador tea, rhodora, the laurels, bearberry, and the blueberries and cranberries.

LABRADOR TEA
(Ledum groenlandicum)

Description
- low shrub, 1 m or less high
- leaves present, 2 to 5 cm long, dark green and leathery above, densely wooly brown underneath, margins rolled under
- buds small, dried fruit capsules may be present
- twigs slender, hairy; old bark dark, reddish
- fruit capsules at twig end

Habitat
- throughout Nova Scotia, usually wet habitats

Notes
- Labrador tea is the only Nova Scotian evergreen in which the undersurfaces of the leaves are covered with dense, brown wool. It is a shrub of wet areas and is eaten by deer, moose and other wildlife. As the common name suggests, the dried leaves may be added to boiling water and steeped for several minutes to make tea.

185

TWIG

NODE

RHODORA
(Rhododendron canadense)

Description
- low shrub, 1 m or less high, upright branches
- leaf scars orange, clustered near twig ends; single, raised bundle scar
- withered, elliptical leaves may persist
- branches ending in several twigs; twigs upright, yellowish
- old bark peeling, underbark reddish or orange
- terminal (flower) bud large, yellow or pink, oval, pointed
- lateral (leaf) buds small, clustered at twig ends
- seed capsules persist, elongate, split into 5 scales

Habitat
- common throughout Nova Scotia
- swamps, wet woods and pastures, hillsides, roadsides

Notes
- Rhodora flowers in early spring before its leaves unfold. Like its cultivated relatives, its purple flowers provide a colorful display over the spring countryside.

186

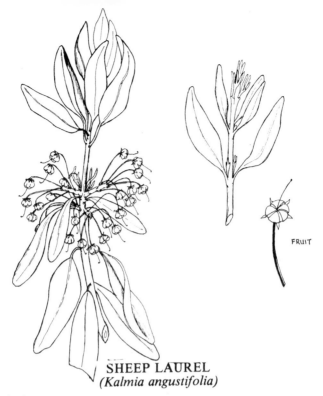

FRUIT

SHEEP LAUREL
(Kalmia angustifolia)

Description
- low shrub, usually less than 1 m, upright branches
- leaves evergreen although withered and leathery, and tinged with red in winter, elliptical in shape, oppositely arranged or in whorls of 3, leaves or leaf scars crowded at end of twigs
- remains of flowers laterally placed along stem
- fruit a capsule, round, usually persisting into winter
- buds minute, twigs smooth

Habitat
- common throughout Nova Scotia, open areas
- fields and pastures, borders, roadsides, hillsides, scrub woodland and woodland trails

Notes
- Sheep Laurel is our most common broadleaf shrub that retains its leaves in winter. It is also called Lambkill because its leaves and twigs are toxic to domestic animals. Pale Laurel *(Kalmia polifolia)* is also found in Nova Scotia. It occurs in bogs and may be distinguished from Sheep Laurel by two characteristics: the remains of the flowers are at the ends of the stems, and the leaves are whitish underneath. The pink and purple flowers bloom throughout spring and much of summer, providing banks of color along our highways and hillsides.

187

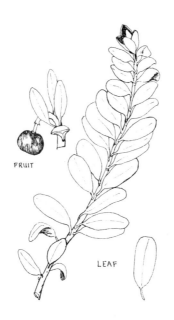

FRUIT

LEAF

BEARBERRY
(Arctostaphylos uva-ursi)

Description
- low trailing shrub, forming dense ground cover
- shiny green leaves present, often brownish with reddish undersurfaces in winter, oval, 1 to 3 cm long
- bark dark brown, old bark peeling, inner bark reddish, twigs hairy

Habitat
- most common in central and western Annapolis Valley, scattered elsewhere
- dry, sandy, open habitats

Notes
- The fruit of Bearberry is berry-like, red, and persists into winter unless eaten by wildlife. As the common name suggests, the berries are a favorite food of bears. They are also eaten by grouse, pheasants, and other wildlife. Tea may be made from the dried leaves.

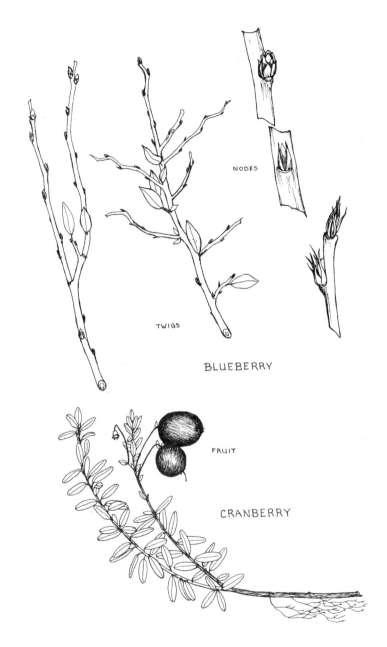

NODES

TWIGS

BLUEBERRY

FRUIT

CRANBERRY

189

BLUEBERRY, CRANBERRY
(Vaccinium, four species)

Description
Blueberry
- low shrubs, crown much branched, forming colonies
- twigs slender, greenish or reddish, rough
- buds small, reddish; leaf buds narrow, flower buds thicker
- leaf scars small, crescent shaped
- leaves elliptical, remaining into winter on some species, withered and brown, sometimes reddish

Cranberry
- low shrub, 15 cm high, forming ground carpet
- stems trailing along ground, short upright twigs
- leaves present, oval, leathery, about 1 cm long, green, sometimes reddish tinge

Habitat
- some species common throughout Nova Scotia
- various habitats; usually open, dry, sandy
- old fields, open woods, barrens, burned areas, roadsides
- cranberries in wet, peat areas

Notes
- Four species of Blueberries are native to Nova Scotia. Others have been introduced and cultivated. The berries of all are edible and of commercial value. Cranberries may be collected, preferably after they have been touched by frost, and used fresh, frozen or dried. Many species of birds and mammals feed on the berries and browse on the twigs of Blueberries and Cranberries.

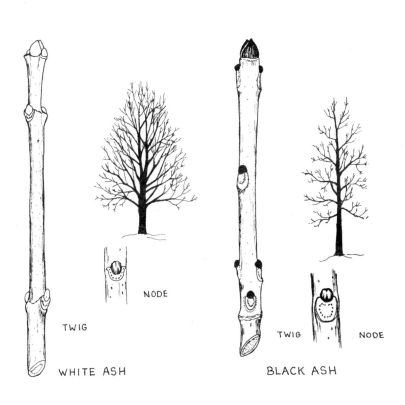

NODE

TWIG

WHITE ASH

TWIG

NODE

BLACK ASH

OLIVE FAMILY

The olive family includes several well-known trees and shrubs such as the olive tree, forsythia and privet. The latter two are frequently planted in Nova Scotia. The ashes and lilac also belong to this family and are included in *Nature Notes*.

ASHES

Three species of ash are native to Nova Scotia, of which two, White Ash and Black Ash, are included in *Nature Notes*. These two may be distinguished in winter, as described below, by the shape of the leaf scars and by the position of the first pair of lateral buds.

WHITE ASH
(Fraxinus americana)

Description
- medium to large tree, straight trunk, young growth may be shrub-like
- buds dark brown, terminal bud rounded, first pair of lateral buds adjacent to terminal bud
- leaf scars prominent and deeply notched below bud
- twigs thick, smooth
- young bark greenish-grey; old bark ash-grey with shallow, branching ridges

Habitat
- throughout Nova Scotia
- along streets and roads, and in mixed, open woods

Notes
- White Ash is found mixed with other hardwoods. It is often planted as an ornamental. Its lumber is used for furniture and interior finishes. White Ash wood is strong and elastic and can bend without breaking. Thus, it is valuable for making tool handles and sporting equipment such as snowshoes, skis, and hockey sticks. The seeds are eaten by many birds, are favourites of grosbeaks, and several mammals browse on the twigs and bark.

BLACK ASH
(Fraxinus nigra)

Description
- small to medium-sized tree, young growth may be shrub-like
- buds black, terminal bud broad and pointed, first pair of lateral buds below level of terminal bud
- leaf scars oval, not deeply notched below bud
- twigs thick, smooth
- young bark grey; old bark furrowed, scaly

192

Habitat
- scattered to rare throughout Nova Scotia, open habitats
- along streams, borders of lakes and swamps

Notes
- Black Ash is also called Basket Ash because its wood is used to make baskets. The wood, after soaking, can be separated along the yearly growth rings. These thin strips are split and used to weave baskets.

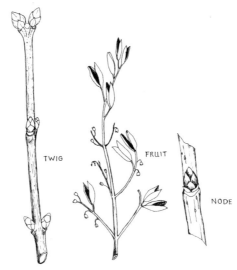

LILAC
(Syringa vulgaris)

Description
- large, upright shrub; older ones may be tree-like
- buds oval, small, not stalked, greenish or reddish, opposite
- terminal buds usually paired, although some varieties have a single small terminal bud
- bundle scars fused to form a straight or curved line, lilac is the only shrub in Nova Scotia with such a bundle scar, can be seen only on the larger leaf scars with a hand lens
- twigs smooth, brown or grey, small white lenticels
- fruit capsules persisting into winter

Habitat
- planted throughout Nova Scotia

Notes
- Lilacs are not native in Nova Scotia, they were introduced as ornamental flowering shrubs. They have spread along roadsides and into the borders of woodlands and are found, frequently forming hedges, near abandoned farms and fields. In the more remote areas, Lilacs mark the sites of former homesteads.

193

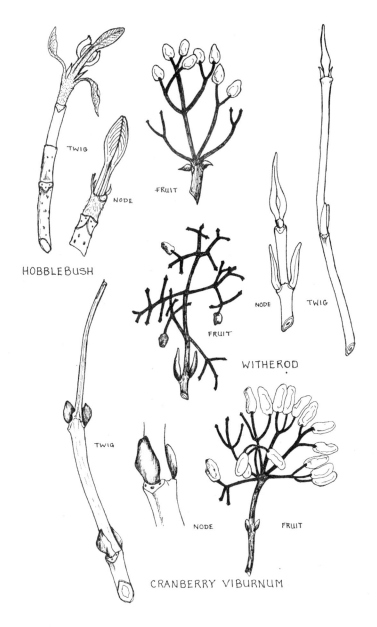

TWIG

NODE

FRUIT

HOBBLEBUSH

FRUIT

NODE

TWIG

WITHEROD

TWIG

FRUIT

NODE

FRUIT

CRANBERRY VIBURNUM

194

HONEYSUCKLE FAMILY

There are several members of the honeysuckle family in Nova Scotia, and ornamental honeysuckles are frequently planted about homes. The viburnums and elderberries are members of this family, are common in our woodlands, and are included in *Nature Notes.*

VIBURNUMS

HOBBLEBUSH
(Viburnum alnifolium)

WITHE-ROD OR WILD RAISIN
(Viburnum cassinoides)

CRANBERRY VIBURNUM
(Viburnum trilobum)

Several Viburnums are native to Nova Scotia or are introduced as ornamentals. The 3 species included here are the ones most likely to be found in the woodlands. All are shrubs with opposite leaf scars having 3 bundle scars, with stalked buds often showing green undeveloped leaves, and with fruit or dried fruit stems present during winter.

Description

Hobblebush - large shrub, less than 3 m; arching branches, some rooting at tips
- buds without scales showing green developing leaves
- twigs hairy, purplish, ending in clusters
- leaf scars broad

Withe-rod - large shrub, less than 2 m
- buds long and narrow, covered with a single pair of yellowish scales, lateral buds curling around stem
- twigs brown, dotted with lenticels
- leaf scars narrow
- fruit blue or black berries, remaining into winter

Cranberry Viburnum - erect shrub, less than 3 m
- buds large, green, covered with 2 overlapping scales
- twigs smooth, greyish, ridged
- leaf scars narrow, fruit red and persisting into winter unless eaten by wildlife
- no terminal buds, end section of twig usually dead

Habitat
- throughout Nova Scotia, Cranberry Viburnum more common in central and northern counties and Cape Breton
- shady and moist habitats, mixed woods, open pastures, borders of streams and lakes

Notes
   - The fruit of the Viburnums is eaten by many species of birds and the twigs are browsed by deer, moose and smaller mammals. Cranberry Viburnum is not a true cranberry but its fruit may be used as a substitute for cranberry. The fruit of the Withe-rod is also edible.

COMMON ELDER
(Sambucus canadensis)
RED-BERRIED ELDER
(Sambucus pubens)

Description
Common Elder - large, open shrub
   - buds small (4mm or less), conical, greenish or brownish scales with black tips
   - single terminal bud absent, replaced by pair of lateral buds
   - leaf scars opposite, narrow, often 5 bundle scars in a V-shaped line
   - twigs stout, angled, large white pith, end of twig often dead
   - lenticels large, raised, round or oval

Red-berried Elder - large, open shrub
   - buds large (10mm), oval, greenish scales edged with purple
   - single terminal bud absent, replaced by pair of buds
   - leaf scars opposite, wide, often 5 bundle scars in a U-shaped curve
   - twigs stout, angled, brown pith
   - lenticels large, raised, oval

Habitat
   - throughout Nova Scotia, damp and open areas
   - abandoned fields, along streams and lakes, woodland clearings

Notes
   - The twigs and fruit of both Elders are eaten by many mammals (a favourite of moose) and birds. Red-berried Elder produces oval-shaped sprays of white flowers in spring and oval clusters of red berries in summer. These are usually lost by winter. Common Elder is an attractive roadside shrub producing flat clusters of white flowers in summer and purple berries in autumn. The dried berry stalks often remain on Common Elder into winter. The berries of Common Elder may be collected in autumn and used to make pies, jellies, and wine.

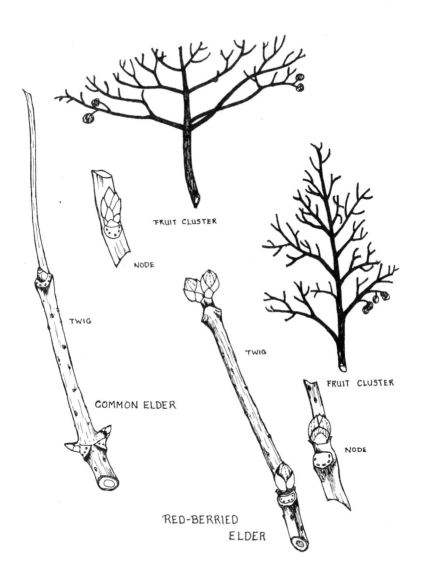

FRUIT CLUSTER

NODE

TWIG

COMMON ELDER

TWIG

FRUIT CLUSTER

NODE

RED-BERRIED
ELDER

CHECK LIST OF TREES AND SHRUBS

The following Check List includes only those trees and shrubs that are described in *Nature Notes*. Some species are distributed throughout the province, others are present in certain localities only. The list is generally restricted to the more common native species although a few introduced ones are also included.

Species	Date First Observed	Location First Observed
Canada Yew (Ground Hemlock)		
Balsam Fir		
Hemlock		
White Spruce		
Red Spruce		
Black Spruce		
Larch (Tamarack)		
White Pine		
Red Pine		
Scotch Pine		
Jack Pine		
White Cedar		
Common Juniper		
Willows		
Trembling Aspen		
Large-toothed Poplar		
Lombardy Poplar		
Balsam Poplar		
Sweet Gale		
Bayberry		
Sweetfern		
Hazelnut		
Ironwood		
Yellow Birch		
Grey (Wire) Birch		
White (Paper) Birch		
Downy Alder		

Species	Date First Observed	Location First Observed
Speckled Alder		
Beech		
English Oak		
Red Oak		
White (American) Elm		
Common Barberry		
Japanese Barberry		
Witch-Hazel		
Meadowsweet		
Steeple-bush		
Apple		
Chokeberry		
Mountain Ash		
Dogberry		
Rowan Tree		
Shadbush (Wild Pear)		
American Hawthorn		
English Hawthorn		
Raspberry		
Dewberry		
Blackberry		
Rose		
Pin Cherry		
Black Cherry		
Choke Cherry		
Honey Locust		
Black Locust		
Clammy Locust		
Staghorn Sumac		
Canada Holly		
False Holly		

Species	Date First Observed	Location First Observed
Mountain Maple		
Striped Maple		
Sugar Maple		
Red Maple		
Silver Maple		
Horse Chestnut		
Bassword (Linden)		
Red Osier Dogwood		
Alternate-leaved Dogwood		
Labrador Tea		
Rhodora		
Sheep Laurel		
Pale Laurel		
Bearberry		
Blueberry		
Cranberry		
White Ash		
Black Ash		
Lilac		
Hobblebush		
Withe-rod		
Highbush Cranberry		
Common Elder		
Red-berried Elder		

ACKNOWLEDGMENTS AND REFERENCES

Sherman Boates, Tom Herman, Sam VanderKloet, and Jim Wolford have generously taken time to read the manuscript of *Nature Notes*. They shared notes from their own observations and offered many helpful suggestions. Dr. R.W. Tufts, well-known authority and writer on birds, read the section on birds and added a number of interesting notes. The assistance of these readers is very much appreciated.

There are many excellent books on nature and I have selected a number to mention here. These are books that I use regularly. I include them as a means of acknowledging their use as references during the preparation of *Nature Notes*. Also, they are recommended for your use should you wish additional reading or more complete "Field Guides".

Birds

1. Godfrey, W. Earl. 1966. *The Birds of Canada.* National Museums of Canada. Ottawa, Ontario

2. Peterson, Roger Tory. 1947. *A Field Guide to the Birds.* Houghton Mifflin Company, Boston.

3. Robbins, C.S., B. Bruun, and H. S. Zim. 1966. *Birds of North America.* Golden Press. New York.

4. Tufts, Robie W. 1973. *The Birds of Nova Scotia.* Nova Scotia Museum. Halifax, Nova Scotia.

Mammals

5. Banfield, A.W.F. 1974. *The Mammals of Canada.* National Museums of Canada. Ottawa, Ontario

6. Burt, William H. 1957. *Mammals of the Great Lakes Region.* The University of Michigan Press. Ann Arbor, Michigan.

7. Burt, William H. and Richard P. Grossenheider. 1964. *A Field Guide to the Mammals.* The Peterson Field Guide Series. Houghton Mifflin Company. Boston.

8. Cameron, Austin W. 1972. *Canadian Mammals.* National Museums of Canada. Ottawa, Ontario.

9. Godin, Alfred J. 1977. *Wild Mammals of New England.* The John Hopkins University Press. Baltimore and London.
10. Murie, Olaus J. 1975. *A Field Guide to Animal Tracks.* The Peterson Field Guide Series. Houghton Mifflin Company. Boston.

Trees and Shrubs

11. Core, Earl W. and Nelle P. Ammons. 1958. *Woody Plants in Winter.* The Boxwood Press, Pacific Grove, California.
12. Hosie, R.C. 1979. *Native Trees of Canada.* Canadian Forestry Service, Department of the Environment, Information Canada, Ottawa.
13. Donly, James F. 1960. *Identification of Nova Scotia Woody Plants in Winter.* Bulletin No. 19. Nova Scotia Department of Lands and Forests.
14. Petrides, George A. 1972. *A Field Guide to Trees and Shrubs.* The Peterson Field Guide Series. Houghton Mifflin Company. Boston.
15. Roland, A.E. and E.C. Smith. 1969. *The Flora of Nova Scotia.* The Nova Scotia Museum. Halifax, N.S.
16. Saunders, Gary L. 1970. *Trees of Nova Scotia.* Nova Scotia Department of Lands and Forests.

INDEX

Part 1: BIRDS

Part 2: MAMMALS

Part 3: TREES AND SHRUBS